P9-DUU-284

UNCORRECTED PAGE PROOF

For review purposes only. Not for sale.

For more information, please contact:

Colleen Lanick
The MIT Press
55 Hayward Street
Cambridge, MA 02142

617 253-2874
colleenl@mit.edu

Subrights contact:

Cristina Sanmartín
617 253 0629
csan@mit.edu

Title: *The More We Know*

Authors: Eric Klopfer and Jason Haas

Probable Publication Date: October 2012

Probable Price: $27.95 cloth

ISBN: 978-0-262-01794-7

Pages: 224 / 46 Illustrations

Size: 7 x 9.5

The More We Know

The More We Know

NBC News, Educational Innovation, and Learning from Failure

Eric Klopfer and Jason Haas

foreword by Henry Jenkins

The MIT Press
Cambridge, Massachusetts
London, England

MIT Press books may be purchased at special quantity discounts for business or sales promotional use. For information, please email special_sales@mitpress.mit.edu or write to Special Sales Department, The MIT Press, 55 Hayward Street, Cambridge, MA 02142.

This book was set in Stone Sans and Stone Serif by Toppan Best-set Premedia Limited, Hong Kong. Printed and bound in the United States of America.

Library of Congress Cataloging-in-Publication Data
••

10 9 8 7 6 5 4 3 2 1

Contents

Foreword

Henry Jenkins

Three immovable objects walked into a bar. The first was the current world of corporate media (and especially what remains of traditional network news), the second was the current world of higher education (as it lurches toward new funding models and institutional practices), and the third—perhaps the most immovable and intractable of them all—was the current policy and institutional mess we call public education (which is shaped by a profound mismatch between what we know of how students learn and policies that set standards that in no way reflect those insights). Each wanted to buy the others a drink, give them something that might ease their stress, soothe their tempers, or at least let them forget their problems. But they couldn't agree on what the ingredients of this beverage should be, or how it should be paid for, or how they should decide what it should contain, or what kind of relationship would be implied by the buying and selling of drinks, or in what order they should be drinking, or anything else.

(Imagine there's a punchline somewhere around here.)

This is the story of the book you hold in your hand, reduced to the level of a farce—as in, you'd best keep laughing in order to keep from crying. But of course, the iCue saga is more than a farce. It might also be called a tragedy, in which the best of intentions are waylaid, distorted, and brought low through a series of fatal flaws that prevent each of these institutions from fully embracing change, that block them from seeing the future that the others see so clearly, or that require them to sell out what they value the most if they are going to make any progress. Yet calling the story you are about to read a tragedy is to imply that it was a perfect failure from start to finish.

And we all know that nothing's perfect.

In fact, as *The More We Know* makes clear, there were many localized successes along the way, and as a consequence of the efforts described herein, other good things have happened. It is rather a story about imperfect failures and imperfect successes, and about unintended consequences, unreached goals, and unanticipated results.

It is also an epic, involving a constantly changing cast of characters, each embodying—as the characters in any good epic do—the contradictions of their times and featuring multiple heroes who push great boulders up to the tops of high hills, only to watch them roll back down again.

The More We Know is also an adventure story set on the bleeding edge of innovation and reform, one that will offer some guideposts for those of you who would follow in the protagonists' footsteps. There are relatively few postmortems on how great ideas and good intentions do not always turn out the way we expect. I would probably put this on my bookshelf next to Brenda Laurel's *Utopian Entrepreneur*, which describes the rise and fall of Purple Moon and the girls' game movement, or perhaps Sandy Stone's account of working at Atari in its early days. It certainly, as the authors suggest, provides a personal and extended example to illustrate some of what Ito has told us about the creation of educational software or what Allan Collins and Richard Halverson have suggested about the resistance of educational institutions to new technologies and practices.

I am, at best, a minor character in the story you are about to read. I was there at the start, said a few words, soon departed from the picture, and left to read about what happened in the pages of this book like everyone else. From this vantage point, I can testify to the truth and wisdom contained in these pages and bear witness to the sweat, blood, and tears our protagonists shed along the way. Whatever its genre, *The More We Know* is the story of the people in the trenches on the front lines of media change and the authors, themselves key participants, tell it very well here.

I still remember vividly the meeting in the Stella Conference Room, where the authors choose to start this story, and recall the excitement of all involved (as well as the wobbly sensation you get from staring too long as those undulating and multicolored walls). Everyone involved believed that he or she was taking the first step on an exciting new journey, which might help bring some cutting-edge research out of the academic world and into contact with those who had the power to make things happen. Never mind that our paths, in the end, took us in different directions; there should be many more such meetings and many more moments when we can see our agendas aligned.

Those early conversations were informed by a research and pedagogical philosophy that had been taking shape within our MIT community for several years—what William Uricchio and I were calling applied humanities. Those living in the early twenty-first century were in the midst of a period of profound and prolonged media change that was to transform every aspect of our lives. Traditional approaches were going to fail us, and what would especially doom us was if everyone remained locked in separate silos, unable to communicate with one another. Changes were coming from every direction at once, and a broad array of expertise was needed if we were meaningfully going to weather the storm.

Housed in the School of Humanities, Arts, and Sciences, the Comparative Media Studies (CMS) program sought to surf those waves and, in the process, to define a new model for humanities education. Insofar as these changes were as much social and cultural as they were technological, those of us in the humanities had a central role to play in informing our collective choices. But we could play that role only if we, too, escaped the box we had constructed around ourselves. Humanists needed to embrace a more applied vision—one that was open to the public, in conversation with members of industry and policy makers, accessible in its language and pragmatic in its approach.

We hoped that our students would become "thought leaders" for industry, the arts, journalism, education, and public policy—great communicators who could translate the theoretical and historical vocabulary they had acquired through their liberal arts education into resources that might ground their analyses of contemporary phenomena and principles that might empower them to make meaningful changes within a range of different institutional settings. In the course of their careers, they would change jobs many times, often moving across what once would have seemed distinct media or sectors, so they needed to rely on the humanities as a compass that might guide their choices.

We felt strongly that this vision was consistent with the legacy of MIT, that we were walking in the footsteps of Norbert Wiener, Vannevar Bush,

Doc Edgerton, Minor White, Ithiel de Sola Pool, Ricky Leacock, Sherry Turkle, Noam Chomsky, and Nicholas Negroponte, among others, each of whom in his or her own way had sought to make MIT the place where people turned when they wanted a vision for the future of media.

At MIT, what we wanted to do was to create a lab culture for the humanities. The Games to Teach Project and, later, the Education Arcade were among a number of different initiatives that started from this same premise: that, as humanists, we knew things that had been missing from the larger conversation about media change, that we owed it to our students and to the world to roll up our sleeves and apply what we knew through experimentation and entrepreneurship, and that by combining what took place in the lab and what took place in the classroom, we offered a unique set of educational opportunities to the graduate and undergraduate students who passed through our program.

Realizing that vision involved putting ideas on the public agenda through our blogs and podcasts and through public events, such as the Education Arcade convening at the Electronic Entertainment Expo, that are discussed here. Doing so also involved consulting behind the scenes, helping shape the development of new initiatives, helping turn our research into real-world interventions. We were not going to be satisfied doing prototypes and writing them up in journals and walking away, which is all too often what happens when academics in our respective fields try to do applied research. For a long time, academics had difficulty getting a space to be heard at the Game Designers' Conference, because the organization had a long-standing policy of not allowing speakers to talk about games that were not yet completed, a policy designed to prevent its members from touting "vaporware," shilling for titles that still needed another round of funding. Academics, by their very nature, were relegated to the list of those who were trying to "con" the organization's members, because our "products" were merely "thought experiments" that were never going to be finished, never going to enter the marketplace. We wanted to use our knowledge to make a difference in the world and, in the process, show our students that it was possible to be agents of change in their future professions.

Alex Chisholm, who emerges as one of the heroes of this book, was a key architect of this vision. It took shape as he and I traveled together across the country, presenting the ideas to many different potential partners, tacking them to many contemporary developments, refining them for diverse audiences, and trying to figure out what they meant—project by project, student by student. Together, Alex and I talked to industry leaders, for example, about what they valued about liberal arts educations (creativity, vision, cultural understanding) and what they did not (leadership, teamwork, brainstorming, design, real-world applications, project completion), and together, we sought to imagine how we might do the humanities differently. I know that this process shaped my own writing and teaching across the past decade—both at MIT and now at the University of Southern California—in ways that I will never fully be able to understand or acknowledge. There have been times that the world gave me more credit for this than I've deserved; there have been, if I am honest, times when I have taken more credit than was due me, so I am really glad to read an account of these experiences that places Alex Chisholm at the center of what unfolded. Alex lives between worlds—one foot in industry, one foot in the academy, always trying to move them toward greater contact with each other. One minute Alex is a burst of enthusiasm, and the next a storm cloud of anger, but in both of these modes he is a force to be dealt with, and it is his energy and spirit that pushed all of us to do more than we ever would have imagined possible.

The changes we imagined were achieved by a remarkable team of researchers who helped our students build a bridge between the theoretical traditions of the humanities and the application of those ideas in real-world contexts. This book gives you a glimpse of such hard-working researchers as Kurt Squire, Eric Klopfer, Philip Tan, and Scot Osterweil, who were key leaders in our games research program, and there were others working to apply our ideas to education, digital humanities, and civic media. iCue was perhaps the most ambitious initiative to emerge from our effort to build a "lab culture for the humanities." So it is no surprise that the academics, unaccustomed to running with the wolves and swimming with the sharks, lost control at various points in the process and that what emerged only imperfectly reflects the research that inspired it. But the project would never have been launched if there were not folks working in the CMS labs who were true believers in applied humanities.

And, of course, for the whole thing to work, we needed strong industry partners—people who were ready to take the risk of imagining and acting on a different relationship with the academic world, people who knew that industry itself was facing new kinds of problems and that they didn't have all the answers they needed in-house. One of the most valuable aspects of this book for me is that it shows people in the industry balancing interests and gives us some insight into when and how the "bottom line" enters into the equation. It shows people trying to do "the right thing," whether out of a vision for the future of their industry or the future of their society, but having to justify the choices they make to other layers of the company on the basis of cost-benefit analysis. This is a more nuanced picture than we often get of the "political economy" of the creative industries, as is the image we get here of different divisions of the same company pursuing somewhat different agendas, rather than everything working like a well-oiled machine that always knows and always pursues its own interests. Once you get inside "the belly of the beast," corporate America looks more like a dysfunctional family than like the all-knowing entity that emerges in some academic accounts.

Looking back at the end of a decade-plus spent actively pursuing our vision of an applied, interventionist humanities, I still think we were moving in the right direction, perhaps a bit ahead of our time, perhaps flying too much in the face of institutional imperatives and disciplinary biases, certainly ruffling the feathers of faculty members who think that the humanities should judge the world from a more lofty perch rather than getting into the muck with everyone else. We enjoyed remarkable success in terms of conceptual breakthroughs, innovative projects, and students who have moved rapidly to leadership positions in a range of different fields. But the path was never simple and direct, and we faced obstacles on all sides—from within MIT's institutional practices, which were never set up to support this kind of experimentation and innovation within the humanities; from the commercial sector, which has never learned to value adequately the cultural expertise of the academic world; or from the bureaucracies of higher education, which have been created to withstand most outside pressures for change.

In our classrooms, we were teaching our students that media change takes place through evolution rather than revolution, but in our labs, we still wanted to change the world; we wanted to blow down the walls and reshape core institutions; and we were painfully, awkwardly, sweetly naïve. The path forward turned out to be harder than idealists predicted but not nearly so difficult as skeptics and cynics might insist.

The book you hold in your hand describes some of the walls we hit and the ways our faculty, research staff, and students worked around and through them. My hope is that readers will take from this the right set of lessons. We succeeded sometimes, failed sometimes, and learned a great deal always about what it takes to make change in the imperfect world around us. *The More We Know* is not a warning to "avoid this path—there be monsters here"; it is a challenge to "follow us if you dare."

Preface

For more than a decade, we and many of our colleagues have attempted to make sense of how to make the most of the digital technologies and the ease of massive networking that have made our era unlike any prior age for educational purposes. Many have observed the culturally significant pockets of discourse and learning that emerged as the Internet and other technologies such as digital games and cheap video-editing software came of age. Young people have sought out a variety of media and learning experiences, exciting researchers who are predisposed to believe that most children are interested in learning—even those who may not do particularly well in school. These situated, self-directed learning experiences should almost certainly be the antidote to the proscriptive, heavily tested schools that seem to be ruining national curricula and classroom morale while finding inventive new ways to leave children behind.

For our part, we are interested in helping formal education evolve to make the most of these technologies in ways that are both innovative and not so innovative. (We are at an institute of technology, after all.) In part, we believe that this means working on innovations, but that it also means putting innovations through their paces on a larger scale. It is simply not enough to build the better mousetrap—you need to get it out there. This book, then, is a story of scaling. We detail the vagaries of partnering with a particular national media entity, the features of our innovation, and the lessons and consequences of this collaboration, both predictable and not.

The purpose of telling this story is not to propose some radical twist on the good work already being done in proposing new media curricula by folks such as Richard Halverson, Allan Collins, Douglas Thomas, and John Seeley Brown. Neither is the purpose to reveal deep insights into youth media practice as Ito and her colleagues have done. This is a cautionary tale and a tale of celebration and encouragement for all those on either side of the great academic/corporate divide who have good ideas. We are sharing our tale in hopes that others will avoid the same pitfalls, as well as find inspiration in the successes that emerged from this endeavor.

The More We Know begins with two groups of people with troubling but somewhat different problems: NBC News and the MIT Education Arcade, which want to find a young audience and to work at a larger scale, respectively. It covers five years of change in both organizations. This change was all brought about through a single product. The process of creating the educational website iCue allowed both of these players to push into unfamiliar territory, including that of the other organization. Both groups changed and grew considerably in the process through taking risks and believing in lofty possibilities. This book follows the product and both of our organizations from the beginning of our collaboration in 2006 until the present. It explains why both groups were ready to step out of their comfort zones in order to work together and bring the emergent product, iCue, into being. We will track what iCue became as it juggled the threefold concerns of audience, revenue, and market, as well as why we think that story is important. Along the way, we will also connect this project to other, similar endeavors to add perspective and link it to the ideas and research of diligent scholars.

The voice of *The More We Know* may seem strange, as it is at times a history of science and technology, at times the design history of an intervention (see Hoadley 2002), and at times a first person tell-all, like Brenda Laurel's *Utopian Entrepreneur* (2001). We mix these voices (we hope successfully) because we feel the story needs to be told in this way. iCue was not developed in a vacuum, so it is necessary to illuminate its connections to the educational technology that came before it. But the design decisions that were made, either deliberately or through project inertia, are a crucial part of how iCue ended up where it did and why that matters. The details of how all of those decisions were made emerge from the noble, flawed, and deeply human actions of those involved. And we were there.

A learned scholar asked us, in the early stages of this book, "If this is a case study, what is it a case of?" *The More We Know* is an attempt to illuminate how people in a diversity of roles and organizations might begin to help young people make sense of our collective past and the rapidly accumulating data of the "petaflop era" and what the barriers are, both systemic and cultural. This is a book for people with skin in the game.

A note on participant quotations: Throughout this book, we employ a great deal of quoted material from the extensive interviews conducted specifically for this volume. These interviews were conducted by phone and in person with Alex Chisholm, Soraya Gage, Adam Jones, Michael Levin, Mark Miano, Beth Nissen, and Nicola Soares between June 2009 and December 2010. To avoid the constant interruption of lengthy interview citations, which we feel would decrease the readability of the book, we are including this note here. To distinguish between material collected through interview and those collected through primary documents, such as email, we will make those distinctions in the text itself.

Acknowledgments

This book would not have been possible without the hard work, vision, and honesty of the team that made iCue, including Alex Chisholm, Soraya Gage, Adam Jones, Michael Levin, Mark Miano, and Beth Nissen—and their willingness to work with us. We'd like to thank Henry Jenkins for his groundbreaking work that kicked off iCue and also for kicking off our book with the foreword.

We were heavily assisted in the detailed data analysis found in chapter 10 by James K. L. Hammerman and Candy Miller. A more detailed view of this data appears in a shared article in the *International Journal of Learning and Media*.

We had much additional help wrestling the ideas contained herein into book form from many Learned Scholars who gave feedback from afar along the way, including Barry Fishman and Kurt Squire, as well local Learned Scholars Jennifer Groff, Wendy Huang, Eli Meir, Scot Osterweil, Judy Perry, Louisa Rosenheck, Josh Sheldon, and Dana Tenneson. We'd also like to thank Learned APA Scholar Lauren McNamara for her help with the references.

Eric would like to thank his wife, Rachel, for her never-ending support for his academic pursuits across many years and for motivating him to keep improving himself and his work. He would also like to thank his kids, Oren and Maya, for tutoring him in the ways of millennial kids and for making his dreams of educating the next generation a reality; and to thank his parents and in-laws for their shared experience in teaching and learning.

Jason would like to thank his wife, Jessica, for her patience, support, and crazy dances throughout this process. He would also like to thank his family for making him who he is and for their endless support and love. To all the friends whose parties, improv shows, and game nights he missed—hey, he'll be at the next thing. Thanks for being cool about it.

1 Media Education for the Twenty-First Century

You could hear a pin drop in 7-338, the Stella Conference Room at MIT. Alex Chisholm, an MIT learning and media specialist, had just shown a clip from *The Daily Show* to a room filled with NBC News executives and producers and games/learning/new media experts from MIT and the University of Wisconsin. What little laughter there was during the segment, and any trace echoes of that laughter, have died out. It is quiet.

The Stella Room is named after painter Frank Stella. The room is ringed by his *Loohooloo*, an extremely vibrant floor-to-ceiling painting with three-dimensional protrusions and bright, unusual colors. It must be seen to be believed. The small image that we've captured here (figure 1.1) doesn't do it justice. If you can't Google up an image for yourself, it might be helpful to imagine the aurora borealis rendered by an especially imaginative kindergartener with access to neon-colored paints. The oddity of the room, however, was no match for the oddity of the meeting taking place within its curvy walls. Still, in the quiet, *Loohooloo* is the only thing in the room that is LOLing.

The clip Chisholm showed had aired only a few weeks before this meeting. The segment was a thorough dressing-down of contemporary broadcast news and the superficial ways in which serious issues get addressed. Chisholm showed it because he was making the case for a new direction for broadcast news, and to do it he had to draw in sharp relief where its younger audience was going. A survey from the Pew Research Center for the People & the Press had already shown in 2004 (Pew 2004) showed that more young people get their news from *The Daily Show* than from broadcast—the writing was already on the wall, and Chisholm was rubbing it in. Broadcast's audience had been in steady decline since the early 1980s, and the median age of its viewership was sixty (Pew 2004).

Figure 1.1
The Stella Room at MIT, and *Loohooloo.*

NBC was looking for a way to reach younger viewers, fast; Chisholm believed he had the answer.

The idea that Chisholm was pitching, at times called DOTZ, Clutch, or Project Wildfire (among other names), would come to be called iCue when developed by NBC. The project was to meld the attributes of popular social networking sites such as MySpace (Facebook was still deeply restricted at the time), the popularity of online video such as YouTube, and online gaming such as Bejeweled into one multimedia site that would allow young people to connect archival media content to the content they were investigating in coursework in US history, government, and politics, as well as English language and composition. Chisholm was proposing that in order to find a young audience, you have to meet it where it lives.

It should be noted that 2006 was a pretty exciting time for new media—and for the people in the room. On the NBC side, NBC News had just anointed a new CFO, Adam Jones. Jones came from a background in managing new media and, more important, had a reputation for creating effective bottom lines for companies that were struggling. It was hoped that Jones could bring these skills to bear in order to pull NBC News's bacon from the proverbial fire. At NBC generally, the fall lineup was brimming with some exciting new properties as well. Ben Silverman, founder of Reveille Productions, was promoted to head of programming, and shows such as *Heroes, 30 Rock,* and *Studio 60 on the Sunset Strip* were all on offer. Perhaps even more exciting for NBC, Silverman was going to save broadcast television and its advertising model by making an end run around the prominence of digital video recorders. Silverman's model allowed advertisers to pay to have their products embedded in the content of the programs themselves. The episode of *The Office* where Michael Scott hands out the Dundie awards at Chili's? That's Silverman at work.

NBC was doing other things to accommodate new technologies as well. Its network was the first to put complete episodes of its shows online for free, with minimal advertising intrusion (this would foreshadow its early participation in the full-episode video site Hulu). It was posting a comic book online for its show *Heroes*, a "transmedia" practice that reflected the beginning of sharing its intellectual property—its content—across platforms to involve users in new ways.

While NBC was noticing fundamental changes in its viewership and trying to accommodate them, the world was also noticing the rapidly changing landscape of the Internet. The phrase "Web 2.0" was not quite cliché yet and in fact aptly described the transition that was happening across the Internet—a transition from the distribution of content to the provision of services. People, particularly young people, were flocking to participate the Internet in many ways. Social networking, blogs, and sites filled with user-generated content were novel and flourishing. According to Hitwise (Tancer 2006), in July 2004 MySpace had around 0.1 percent of all website visits. By the middle of 2006, MySpace had usurped Yahoo! as the top website, approaching nearly 5 percent of all website visits—nearly a fiftyfold jump in less than two years, making it a powerful player in the market and foreshadowing the even greater growth to come in social networking.

Of course, MySpace's user base was not drawn from every demographic online. According to the Pew Internet and American Life Project (Horrigan 2006), a little more than half of teens were on social networking sites, half of eighteen- to twenty-nine-year-olds were on social networking sites, and only 15 percent of thirty- to forty-nine-year-olds were on such sites. Almost half of teens were on there once a day or more. Of the teens on those sites, 85 percent were on MySpace and a mere 7 percent on Facebook. (This was not yet the Facebook we know today. It was open only to everyone thirteen years and older after September 26, 2006 [Abram 2006]. Before then, it was relegated to graduates and attendees of elite universities and high schools. This was a different landscape than the one today, in which Facebook is a more-dominant player across age categories.) By August 2006, MySpace had registered its 100 millionth account and was already owned by Rupert

Murdoch's News Corporation, which had purchased MySpace in July 2005 for $580 million (Sicklos 2005).

Teens—people of all ages—were still using the Internet in many Web 1.0 ways (information gathering), and they were using it more and more as their primary source of information. Three quarters of teens got news online in 2006, according to (Lenhart et al. 2007). Among eighteen- to twenty-nine-year-olds, in 2007 there was still a gap between Internet (34 percent) and television (68 percent) viewing as a main source of news, but that gap would close entirely by 2008 (Pew Research Center for the People and the Press 2011). On the video front, 57 percent of teens were watching video (Lenhart et al. 2007) on sites such as YouTube (which had been bought by Google in August 2006). Games had already become widely used (67 percent of teens reported playing games) and their use was increasing on sites across the Internet. Forty-nine percent of teens reported playing games online, and that percentage dropped off only slightly for eighteen- to twenty-nine-year-olds, down to 43 percent (Lenhart, Jones, and Macgill 2008). In the intervening years, we have seen those numbers grow, particularly for the older audience.

This exciting and rapidly changing landscape on the Internet is what led our colleague Henry Jenkins and some other researchers here at MIT to embark on a white paper for the MacArthur Foundation, *Confronting the Challenges of Participatory Culture: Media Education for the 21st Century*. For many people, this was the paper that established how we should be teaching teens both with and about media. The paper was released in the fall of 2006 and remains one of the most influential papers in this field. Jenkins and his colleagues define four forms of participatory culture (Jenkins et al. 2006):

Affiliations—memberships, formal and informal, in online communities centered on various forms of media (such as Friendster, Facebook, message boards, metagaming, game clans, or MySpace).

Expressions—producing new creative forms (such as digital sampling, skinning and modding, fan videomaking, fan fiction writing, zines, mash-ups).

Collaborative problem-solving—working together in teams, formal and informal, to complete tasks and develop new knowledge (such as through Wikipedia, alternative reality gaming, spoiling).

Circulations—Shaping the flow of media (such as podcasting, blogging).

At the time, Affiliations was fast becoming the lingua franca for teens, as seen in the number of participants in MySpace. Expressions and Circulations were reaching a comparative but still substantial minority (Lenhart and Madden 2005), with 19 percent of teens writing blogs (Circulations) and 33 percent sharing things that they had created online (Expressions). Teens were online, many of them actively so, but only a fraction of those were fully engaging in participatory culture; this defined what Jenkins called the "participation gap." Some were really excelling and fully participating in media production, creative expression, and collaboration, while many others were only partial participants, dabbling in social networking and consuming information. This latter point has been especially well developed by Ito and colleagues in *Hanging Out, Geeking Out, and Messing Around: Kids Living and Learning with New Media* (2009) and Seiter in *The Internet Playground: Children's Access, Entertainment, and Mis-Education* (2007), among others.

In order to engage more teens in a participatory culture, Jenkins advocated for the increased identification and promotion of what Jim Gee had earlier deemed "affinity spaces" (2003). Affinity spaces are informal (and often online) learning environments in which people with a common interest gather to further their knowledge, understanding, and engagement with the topic of interest. These may be communities of hobbyists blogging and commenting about new products in gardening, or fans of a TV show discussing the latest plot lines in online forums, or political activists mashing up news feeds and maps to comment on government policy. People go to these groups because they are personally interested in the topics being discussed, and they participate because they want to have their voices heard but also want to hear the voices of others. Communities may or may not coalesce, but the result is a group of self-motivated learners that allows people of different levels of expertise to teach and to learn.

Jenkins further notes the relevance of these affinity spaces for engaging young people in politics and civic issues. Despite their active participation online at the time, young people were almost entirely removed from political and civic issues, seeing them as things that adults do. This view was only reinforced by the way that most television and even online news media represented political issues. Jenkins envisioned that creating new affinity spaces, particularly around games, could reengage young people in these important issues.

Politics, as constructed by the news, becomes a spectator sport, something we watch but do not do. Yet, the new participatory culture offers many opportunities for youth to engage in civic debates, to participate in community life, to become political leaders, even if sometimes only through the "second lives" offered by massively multiplayer games or online fan communities . . . . Today's children learn through play the skills they will apply to more serious tasks later. The challenge is how to connect decisions in the context of our everyday lives with the decisions made at local, state, or national levels. The step from watching television news and acting politically seems greater than the transition from being a political actor in a game world to acting politically in the "real world." (Jenkins et al. 2006, 10)

The big idea here—that games, media, and online communities could come together to promote engagement with news and the political process—was a transformational one, a new way forward for presenting the news to young people and engaging them with it. The news is not something you read in isolation, but rather something that you participate in with a community, or at least with others (as opposed to alone). But this wasn't happening in schools. Instead, No Child Left Behind, the 2001 federal act mandating "accountability" in the form of strict standards and regular testing, had firmly taken hold. Educational accountability was being managed largely through ubiquitous testing, often in the form of straightforward multiple-choice and short-answer exams that were not particularly effective at capturing any of these twenty-first-century practices. In response, schools had largely failed to incorporate new ideas such as new media literacies, not because they necessarily disagreed with them, but because that is not what they were accountable for; they couldn't spend time and resources on those skills.

Although it may not have immediately transformed schools, the New Media Literacies paper for MacArthur (Jenkins et al., 2006) transformed the ideas of many, and it had other repercussions as well. It received a great deal of press and brought a spotlight onto the work going on at MIT. Jenkins's book *Convergence Culture* (2006) had also just come out. *Convergence Culture* describes the meeting of old media and new media, theorizing that new media will not simply supplant the old but rather connect with it in new and interesting ways. This concept set the stage, for example, for Chisholm's thinking about new ways in which news video might connect with games and participatory spaces, leveraging both the new and the old.

Of course, this idea was not confined to news media—entertainment television, for example, was also set to capitalize on this convergence, bringing together web-based content with television shows.

The spotlight shining on MIT brought with it a lot of enthusiasm about making a difference in the field of media, games, and young people, beyond the borders of campus. Our research group at MIT, the Education Arcade, had been launched from Jenkins's Games to Teach project, which explored the educational potential of different genres of video games in particular academic areas.

In sum, there was tremendous interest, expertise, and enthusiasm at MIT for a big project that could reach a lot of people and instantiate the ideas that we had been working on already on a small scale. Although the games and media that we had created as research projects might reach thousands or tens of thousands of people over a long time, working with a commercial partner with high visibility could get those numbers up by orders of magnitude in a short time.

So this Stella Room meeting seemed momentous to all involved. After the quiet subsided, both sides agreed that something could be done in this space and that they would do it together. NBC News showed up with its CFO, with high-level news producers, with advisors and an accountant. MIT brought professors of education and of comparative media studies and of computer science (and, of course, graduate students). These two groups from fairly different worlds were convinced that the new world was here and that together they could produce something of value—something of that new world.

SPOILER ALERT: It didn't work. The innovation that emerged from the Stella Room meeting, iCue, debuted to a great deal of interest—the *New York Times* published an early article, and the site received a number of favorable online reviews from technologists and educators. The site that debuted in the summer of 2008 was a far cry from the site imagined in the Stella Room, however. It developed a small audience and saw little traffic over its short life. In the two years that iCue was in production, it fell prey to any number of traps inherent in stepping from one world into another. NBC News would hire a large number of linear producers who were good at telling linear stories but were nervous about letting viewers interpret events for themselves or participate fully in its content through practices such as remix. MIT would trip over itself trying to find a sustainable way to bring its considerable expertise in youth media practice to bear in the design of the site while maintaining the objectivity needed to study the site down the road. Further, the market for an innovation such as iCue was elusive—would teens use this site on their own? Were teachers the market instead, as connectors who could show students a new way to conduct their studies? NBC tried again and again to find the right business partners to take the leap with it, but rarely found much success. For instance, the content in iCue was initially supposed to come from as many sources as possible so that users could have a rich experience evaluating primary documents surrounding an event, but getting access to the archives of any number of news providers proved fruitless.

We see educational technology and learning games on the precipice of another "2006" moment, where companies are looking to get in on an estimated $500 billion market through acquisitions and new endeavors. CEOs and marketers are talking about "gamifying" education, or "iPadify-ing" it, and we hope they read this book first—not just because we think there are important pitfalls to avoid, but because this is not a hopeless tale of a project gone awry. Strange things happen when you try something new. Innovation is rarely born in a string of successes; more frequently, it arises from interesting failures such as this one.

2 The Education Arcade

The Standard Drill

The Education Arcade (TEA) had developed a standard drill by 2005. This "drill" was a way of responding to companies looking to move into educational games. As the promise of video games in education became more widely known, it seemed that just about everyone was trying to get his or her foot in that door. The companies ranged from educational software developers to toy companies to museums. By far, however, most common were the textbook publishers—lots of textbook publishers.

The drill went something like this. An executive from the company would contact Henry Jenkins directly, having either heard him speak or read one of his recent publications. The executive would say that he or she was fascinated by the potential of video games for learning and wanted to move his or her enterprise in that direction. The email would get passed along to others in TEA, notably Alex Chisholm, Kurt Squire (now a professor of education at the University of Wisconsin, Madison), and Eric Klopfer. Chisholm, having the most (meaning any) experience in industry and in interfacing with entities outside academia, would typically be the one to respond.

Chisholm was the consummate man behind the scenes. He had worked at MIT for years, aiding students and raising funds. He provided Henry Jenkins and William Uricchio with important support in the creation of the Comparative Media Studies (CMS) program at MIT. He is addressed in Jenkins's acknowledgments for *Convergence Culture*:

This book emerged from many, many conversations with Alex Chisholm on long drives, early morning waits at airports, and meetings with potential sponsors. While Alex was not always patient with my foolishness, he vetted and refined almost every concept in this book; he taught this humanist how to speak the language of business and, through this process, how to become a better analyst and critic of contemporary media trends. (2006, viii)

Chisholm was crucial to the launch of the CMS program in 2000, navigating for Jenkins and Uricchio the bureaucracy that accompanies new academic initiatives. Once CMS had taken off, Chisholm helped keep it going and broke new ground by seeking out new initiatives. Chisholm could wear fashionable, pressed shirts and talk about value propositions and revenue streams, but also wear a backpack and talk about the latest trends in media theory and education. He was at home in both worlds, yet not really in either of them—when he spoke too much about value propositions he longed for some media theory, and vice versa.

So, back to the drill. Chisholm would respond to the emails, and there would then be exchanges seeking to clarify the executives' interest and see whether it matched with any of the current directions for TEA. The executives obviously knew their stuff. They talked seriously about making video games a significant part of their business moving forward, seeing the great potential of the medium. The possibility of sponsored research (the lifeblood of research faculty) was broached, and the media executives indicated that was a strong possibility. After much wrangling of schedules, we would all meet—the full TEA team would bring out the best Microsoft PowerPoint presentations, demos, and designs, and the media executives would trot out teams of producers, editors, and content experts, who all indicated that their businesses had the need for this fresh input.

The meetings would end with good feelings about great demos and synergy between industry and academia.[1] Next steps were defined, ham-

---

1. CMS is a notable initiative because, unlike traditional university media education programs, it explicitly looks across media and at the connections among media. In many ways this program was far ahead of its time, leading the transmedia phenomenon of today by almost a decade and inspiring hosts of imitators. It is becoming increasingly clear today that understanding culture isn't just about understanding video, print, or the Internet but rather about understanding the connections among these that lead to successful media enterprises—television programs are accompanied by websites that generate buzz and are followed by games that further advance the story, for instance. Almost more important is that CMS has always been interested in climbing into the mud with the producers of culture, whether corporate or not, to understand how culture gets made, and how to improve it if possible, instead of being the scold in the ivory tower.

mering out the "scope of work" (the nature of the work that TEA would do and the associated cost) and running the contract through MIT legal to discuss ownership of intellectual property. The scope of work would slowly decrease with each subsequent volley of emails. There would be sticker shock when the media company saw MIT's overhead rate (the "facilities and administration" rate, which is a "tax" that all universities put on research to cover things that aren't directly budgeted in proposals—utilities, space, departmental administrative support, network access, and so forth). The scope would be further reduced because the executives had trouble justifying the costs for an exploratory project without immediate return on investment. As the scope of work slowly decreased, the work negotiating intellectual property ownership inevitably increased. The media company would want free and exclusive rights to everything that was produced. MIT, accustomed to developing biomedical interventions and aerospace technologies, would want at least joint ownership, and wouldn't take restrictions on the ability of faculty members to publish about the research they were conducting. Finally, when some small fraction of the original scope of work was agreed upon, the project would fall by the wayside due to a legal impasse, change in personnel, or refocusing of core priorities at the media company.

This drill happened frequently enough that we began to call it "free consulting." Most companies were not deeply interested in a partnership with TEA but rather in tapping the expertise of TEA to get some understanding of the new media landscape without having to pay an expert group of consultants. This free consulting not only was frustrating but also wore heavily on the spirits of TEA, sapping resources from a team that was both stretched and looking for the next big thing for when current funding ran out.

Roots

So, just how did TEA become one of the go-to "free consulting" organizations in the area of educational video games? The Education Arcade's roots can clearly be traced back to a previous MIT effort known as Games to Teach (G2T). Games to Teach was the brainchild of Henry Jenkins, and was a part of the Microsoft iCampus initiative started by Microsoft Research in collaboration with MIT in 1999. The goal of iCampus was to spark innovation in educational practices through digital technologies at MIT.

Though most of the work of iCampus focused on the postsecondary classes of MIT and similar institutions, some of the work had implications for elementary and secondary (K–12) education as well. Such was the case for G2T. Chisholm was the critical liaison between the academic mindset of MIT and the corporate mindset of Microsoft Research, which often talked past each other. Even though G2T was connected with the research branch of Microsoft, corporate and academic research were often worlds apart.

Jenkins was the principal investigator of G2T; he was joined early on by Kurt Squire, then a graduate student at Indiana University. Squire had been studying learning through games, and even then was one of the thought leaders in this space. He has since become one of the leading scholars and advocates of learning through both commercial off-the-shelf (COTS) games and games designed specifically for learning. Jenkins and Squire set their sights on reinventing educational games, while also reinventing education through games. The goal of G2T was to go beyond the edutainment-era designs of educational games to create ten educational-game prototypes that deeply integrated sophisticated modern game design with learning. The prototypes spanned different platforms, genres, subjects, and pedagogies, and were specifically mapped out to span that space in as broad a way as possible. Games ranged from multiplayer games about engineering to Xbox games about immunology to role-playing games about the American Revolution.

Games to Teach Games

It is important to note that the prototypes were in the form of designs, screenshots, and walkthroughs, not playable games, which allowed G2T to reframe the discussion of educational games without getting bogged down (at least initially) in the cost and complexity of developing ten games that would require many different types of content area expertise and familiarity with multiple gaming platforms. But to this day, we still get requests for many of the games that were never more than designs on "paper."

After the prototypes were complete, they immediately received a lot of attention. A few of the games were taken beyond the prototype level as a second phase of the G2T funding. Supercharged! was a PC-based game about electromagnetism that was designed for MIT classes, but it was ultimately tested not only at the university level but also in middle school classes (Barnett et al. 2004). Supercharged! was unique at

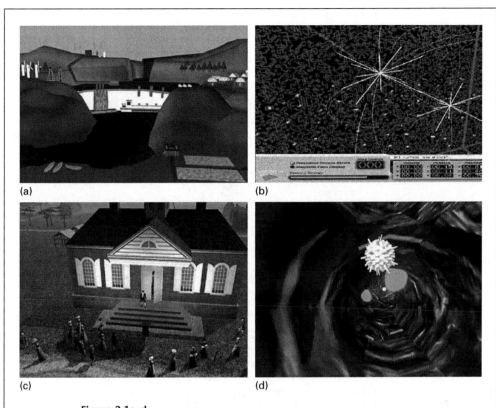

(a)   (b)

(c)   (d)

Figure 2.1a–d
Four of the Games to Teach prototypes (clockwise from upper left)—Daedalus' End, a multiplayer engineering game; Supercharged, a 3D first-person game about electromagnetism; Replicate, a PC/Xbox game about immunology; and Revolution, a multiplayer role-playing game about the American Revolution.

the time for its ambitious approach to educational game development. The combination of 3D first-person play, narration, production, and gameplay put it on par with many noneducational games of the time. That combination came at the cost of complex development, which made it technically fragile. Still, it managed to engage and educate physics students from middle school through university. Environmental Detectives, a mobile game, also was turned into a playable game, and later became the basis for a variety of "augmented reality" games (location-based games played on mobile devices). Although this genre of location-based gaming is now common on cell phones through platforms such as Scvngr and Foursquare, it was at the cutting edge of technology at the time.

First Attempt at Revolution

Another prototype, Revolution, was a historically themed multiplayer game set in Colonial Williamsburg about the role of everyday people in sparking the American Revolution. Philip Tan, who had recently graduated from the CMS program (now the director of the Singapore-MIT Gambit Game Lab), led the project. As an educational game, Revolution offered several innovations. Rather than exploring the role of all of the famous historical figures, as most historical media did, it focused on regular people—blacksmiths, carpenters, slaves, and the like. It was also a multiplayer game, in which up to nine players work with (and against) each other in a locally networked game. Owing to Tan's attention to detail, the game also had extremely high production values, with artwork well beyond the standards of the time.

But Revolution's primary innovations were not apparent by looking at the screen. Instead these innovations focused on how you make high-quality educational games in an economically feasible way and fit them into schools. Supercharged!, like most other educational games at the time, was a game written from the ground up for this project. This production method had the advantage of being able to customize every detail to fit the product, but it increased the cost and complexity of developing everything for the project—the 3D engine, the controls, the scoring display, cut-scenes . . . the list went on. Instead, the design of Revolution was to leverage an existing game engine and modify (or "mod") that game to make it work for its own particular context. The practice of modding was not new, and many games at the time offered tools to sophisticated users to mod their games. Players could introduce new assets or levels or even craft entirely new games. Typically, these mods kept a game within the same genre—so, for example, one might mod a space-based role-playing game to be a different space-based role-playing game.

Revolution took this a step further and attempted to mod Neverwinter Nights, a fairly typical Dungeons and Dragons role-playing game, into an American colonial history game. This task meant getting a lot of features for "free"—game controls, 3D rendering, multiplayer networking. The trade-off was that undesirable features had to be worked around. The "weapons" in Revolution were not swords and maces—these were replaced by information. If players took off all of their "armor" in the game, they'd be thrown in the stocks for streaking. After working around these details, the end product was of professional quality both in production and in software stability, achieved at a reasonable cost.

The second big innovation of Revolution was that it was structured in a series of units, with each game unit lasting no more than forty-five minutes. One of the challenges of getting games into schools is that it is often hard to get students into a game, and then ready to leave it, all within the space of a single class period. Revolution was designed as a series of modules that could be completed within a class period. The students could then begin the next "chapter" during a later class. The first round of funding for Revolution provided resources to develop the first of these chapters and try it out in classes.

The first tests of Revolution were quite successful. The gameplay was top-notch and, despite the perils of modding, provided the experience all had hoped for. It demonstrated a means of producing top educational video games at reduced cost through modding. The real achievement would be in the completion of the project—the development of the remaining chapters. So, in 2003, the negotiations for the next phase of research began with Microsoft Research. The first phase had focused on designs and paper prototypes, the next on proofs of concept; this last phase would be focused on scaling and implementation—getting quality products into the hands of teachers. There were plans to expand the Augmented Reality platform (for Environmental Detectives), but much of this phase would work on developing the rest of the Revolution modules.

The team, including Klopfer, who worked on one of the mobile applications, developed several successful prototypes. (See the box on Games to Teach Games.) However, from the perspective of the Microsoft Research team, once these prototypes were developed, the project had already served its purpose—sparking ideas in the space of educational games. At the time, the team was not interested in increasing the scale of these products, even if the scaling itself (development at reduced costs through modding) was going to be an important part of the equation if the value of educational gaming were going to accepted by the educational establishment. This approach was frustrating for the team at MIT, which still found its work isolated, relegated to academia and small-scale implementations; it seemed like a missed opportunity to stretch those boundaries.

In the wake of G2T, the group set out to redefine itself and rebrand the movement that had become associated with the title of this particular project. Because the group was no longer able to rely on the funding from Microsoft Research, they now also had an opportunity to seek broader alliances with industry. Seeking to start out with a splash, the group aligned with the Entertainment Software Association (ESA), the big trade group for video game companies. This connection came in part due to Chisholm's industry connections, acquired during his time at LeapFrog, and brought together industry experts and academics alike (along with some sponsorship from LeapFrog). That collaboration initially took the form of an educational games meeting (announced in the fall of 2003) immediately before the big Electronic Entertainment Expo (E3) in May 2004. The conference was dubbed the Education Arcade, and gathered games industry standouts such as Will Wright (of SimCity, The Sims, and Spore fame) and Warren Spector (of Ultima, Deus Ex, and System Shock fame), as well as academic leaders such as Jenkins and James Paul Gee (*What Video Games Have to Teach Us about Learning and Literacy*). Of course, there were also representatives from companies such as LeapFrog and representation from the ESA itself.

But the Education Arcade drew in wider representation as well. There was a panelist from *Dateline NBC*, and another from the Royal Shakespeare Company. The vision was not only to inform game design with great work in other media but also to create a vision for how these media might work together. This was the vision that Jenkins saw coming in *Convergence Culture*. *Convergence Culture*'s picture of a new media landscape in which digital technologies were transforming the way people select and interact with media, fueled by interest from digital media professionals but also others with a stake in media. If people no longer merely let media flow to them at preselected times through limited channels, but rather controlled those media through new technologies, influenced those media through discussion, remixed those media through digital tools, and even created and shared those media through the Internet, it meant change for these organizations. Further, the boundaries of particular media were blurring. There were podcasts about books, movies created within video games, and fan fiction about TV characters. Thus, having a vision for the way video games could play a role in learning meant also thinking about the whole ecology of media and participation that came with games.

The conference generated a lot of media attention. It also brought with it the desire to act upon the messages that were being delivered—to form fruitful partnerships between the media industry and academia in the interest of education. A lot of discussion followed, and the effort was deemed a great enough success to hold the conference again at E3 in 2005, again drawing a mix of industry and academia. In parallel, Chisholm was working to connect the industry where he now resided with the work of the Education Arcade back at MIT, still looking for the next big thing to work on.

Re-Rebranding

The Education Arcade itself was doing some soul searching, trying to find its identity. After two years of the Education Arcade at E3, late in 2005 TEA called off the 2006 edition of the conference due to some changes in E3. Although the most significant changes in E3 would come the following year (scaling back from a grand no-expense-spared event to a much smaller and more targeted one), 2006 already saw some scaling back, which left TEA without the partnership of the ESA. New projects started to roll in, capitalizing on the experiences and successes of the event. There were extensions of the Augmented Reality work and a federal grant to produce math games in partnership with Maryland Public Television. The latter was particularly exciting, potentially providing the partnership for the scaling that never came to pass with Revolution.

The leadership of TEA had shifted to Squire (now at the University of Wisconsin), Chisholm (working from the outside), and Klopfer. By this time, the educational games movement had gained significant momentum. The Games, Learning, and Society conference had gone through its first iteration in Madison, Wisconsin. Books and edited volumes seemed to be published monthly on the topic of educational games. But there still seemed to be a gap between the work done at universities and other institutions of learning and what was going on in the media industry. This gap existed not only in their practices, but also in the modes of operation. While the academics were tinkering with new ideas on a small scale, most of the industry practiced as it had for years, slowly seeking out new ideas and directions. With these differences in practice in mind, TEA's mission was to position itself as the glue between the ideas coming from academia and the opportunities that the industry provided. It would reach significant audiences and sustain initiatives for more than the short, funded shelf-life of university-based projects. Though MIT had a history of successful spinoffs and industry collaboration (by some estimates, the economy associated with MIT spinoffs would make it the world's eleventh-largest economy), most of this history was pretty far afield from the domain of educational media that TEA was trying to break into.

Forging Ahead with Media Partnerships

By 2006, Chisholm had made inroads at NBC (an issue we discuss further in the next chapter), and the first real opportunity to collaborate on a larger scale came through the NBC Weather Plus channel (NBC's station dedicated to weather before it acquired the Weather Channel). As a television station, it was required to provide a minimum number of hours of educational programming each week. It was interested in deviating from the more mundane and low-cost productions that it had relied on and instead wanted to think about new products that could drive new audiences to its channel and companion website.

Through a series of conversations and meetings, the MIT and NBC teams wrote a proposal to the National Science Foundation (NSF) to develop a product known as Weather Works. Weather Works was designed to be a website for kids to learn more about and engage with weather, the science behind weather, and the impact of weather. The product was designed at its core to be both transmedia and participatory. There would be games online, applications for cell phones, and connections to television programs that would be produced for the project. The games involved a combination of simulation-style games (e.g., manipulating weather conditions to make it snow in Washington, DC, on New Year's Day) and nowcasting (short-term weather prediction). The nowcasting games involved the formation of communities, because players would compete against others in the same geographic area. There were also competitions involving user-generated content such as pictures and videos of weather phenomena from cell-phone cameras. The television programs would help kids learn about weather phenomena to make them better at the games, and they could ultimately win airtime with the meteorologists at their local NBC affiliates as a prize.

Chisholm wrote the majority of the proposal for Weather Works, balancing the requirements for MIT on the research and development side with the real demands on Weather Works and their deliverables. Navigating these demands would prove to be an instructive challenge, but it was also what made the project interesting. Alas, Weather Works didn't work from the perspective of NSF reviewers, and the project never came to pass.

But the collaboration, even if just on a proposal, was fun, different, and exciting from the TEA perspective. This collaboration meant breaking away from the typical academic models and delving into the world of corporate partnerships with vast reach and (it seemed) vast resources. It was an opportunity to bring ideas outside the laboratory and into the real world, helping fulfill the somewhat academically atypical mission of TEA. The meetings between TEA and NBC Weather Plus were all positive and encouraging, and left TEA wanting to seek out partnerships like that again. This whet the appetite of TEA for media collaboration, and Chisholm was ready to turn the "free consulting" model around.

3 An Education Revolution

The Lights Are Going to Go Out

In 2006, NBC News was in tough shape—perhaps not compared to its broadcast competitors, but in tough shape nonetheless. When NBC Universal implemented massive cuts and layoffs in October 2006 in order to move further into digital space, *USA Today* reported, "For now, the changes will pinch hardest in the company's vast news operations, which include NBC News, MSNBC, CNBC and the 26 company-owned stations" (Lieberman, Johnson, and Levin 2006). It was true that television news was generally in terrible shape, but did it deserve to be the focus of $750 million and seven hundred jobs in cuts?.

The quality was there. *NBC Nightly News* was regularly winning in the ratings and had been for at least two years with Brian Williams as anchor, consistently outpacing ABC and particularly CBS, which had recently experienced losses upon making Katie Couric its new evening anchor. NBC News had a great legacy of quality programming, with *The Today Show* unassailable in the morning and *Nightly News* regularly winning in its slot since the mid-1990s. It was nevertheless, along with its competitors in evening television news, winning a contracting, aging audience. The audience and the formats that it had relied on for decades—the evening news and prime-time news programs—were aging, and it was more and more rapidly losing its audience of young viewers. The situation seemed dire, which led NBC Universal to hire Adam Jones as the new CFO in April 2006.

Jones was a trained financier and a chartered accountant. He had worked for firms as diverse as Price Waterhouse and IMG Sports Management before being headhunted by Universal in 2003. Universal had been under the control of Vivendi, which had botched things quite seriously and then returned control to Universal. The company needed someone to turn around the finances of the Universal International Television Networks group, under Vivendi (Canal +) management, within a year, and a friend at NBC Universal–owned USA Networks suggested Jones. Jones was offered a one-year deal to turn around a business that was losing $60 million. The group had fourteen channels, three of which were in bankruptcy already and most of which were in default with their carriage providers, and it was also the target of four active lawsuits. Jones was forced to lay off 30 percent of the workforce, shut down two of the channels, and renegotiate about a half a billion dollars in carriage deals in nine months. The group was profitable within twelve months.

Indeed, if you haven't guessed yet, Jones, as CFO, was responsible for gutting NBC News in October 2006. Universal was acquired by General Electric during Jones's tenure in Universal International Television, and normally a big corporation such as GE would clean house upon such a major acquisition, but because Jones had essentially worked miracles, he was offered a shot at one of a few of NBC Universal's major CFO jobs back in the United States. During his interview with the president of NBC News, Steve Capus, he said, "Let's be very, very clear that I'm not your typical CFO. And if I come in here and changes need to be made, I will make those changes. I will turn the place upside down. . . . Be aware that if I come here, a lot's going to happen." Jones would make good on his promise.

Jones began his tenure by spending a few weeks meeting the various senior people in the organization, observing the ways the various departments worked, and generally getting a sense of the place. He says, "What I got coming out of that . . . was a profound sense that the business was heading into fairly dangerous waters and wasn't conscious of it. . . . When you analyze [broadcast production] as a business . . . you have a single source of revenue in a declining market, and you have an inexorable and completely unchangeable decline."

Not only was NBC News deeply entrenched in the rapidly diminishing business of broadcast production, its employees were also working against one another. The network's various productions (*Nightly News*, *The Today Show*, and so forth) were considered to be completely separate from one another and would frequently send their own camera crews to cover the same event. As Jones did his research, he couldn't believe the lack of perspective in the building. As the Pew Center for Journalism (Horrigan 2006) reports, the audience for broadcast news was rapidly increasing in age and decreasing in viewership. The decline in total viewership had begun around 1980 and never stopped. Jones predicted, "It will hit zero somewhere around about 2015 for certainly one of the three of the broadcasters. I can see that the lights are going to go out on one of the broadcasters in the next five years, absolutely no question from a news perspective because it's inevitable." Jones took stock of his assets and set about convincing his new colleagues that the current technology trends were going to change the consumer forever.

A Race against the Clock

Jones knew that as part of his plan, he was going to have to capture more of the youth market, and it wasn't happening through the traditional broadcast news venues. Jones saw that his way forward was clear, and he almost immediately set about "throwing bombs down corridors" and telling his new colleagues, "We're about to fall off a cliff." He predicted declines in ratings and revenues if things didn't change. He says, "When you project that out, it was a fairly significant loss of profitability. . . . Literally 2 or 3 percent revenue erosion a year and 5 percent cost inflation. The profits in the business were wiped out in three or four." He knew that the production methods would have to become more cost-effective and that the news stories could no longer be prepared just for the day of broadcast. The production culture would have to change its orientation toward more "on demand," anytime-anywhere formats such as mobile and the Web.

One of the most significant changes that Jones pushed for was to bring MSNBC as a third-party production operation back in to the NBC News studios at 30 Rockefeller Center, moving it from its offices in Secaucus, New Jersey. "That did a number of things, because the cable production sensibility is much more low cost and much more efficient," Jones says. But that move and the cuts in October were going to get him only so far. In addition to replicating his success at Universal International Television in paring back a bloated organization, NBC News was going to have to develop new revenue lines. Recognizing that it already did great production work, Jones decided that the organization would need to focus on expanding that work, becoming a production house for others in addition to its own news work. But Jones was also eyeing the archives. His focus on finding audiences with more "on demand" formats had brought his attention to the company's mountain of dormant intellectual property (which grew after every broadcast day). In its collection were radio pieces from the 1920s and Universal Newsreels from the 1930s and 1940s. Moreover, much of this material was going to expire as the film and magnetic materials on which it resided slowly decayed over time. Making the archives into something reusable—a lossless, digital format—was, in Jones's view, "a race against the clock." The question was how he could, in a cost-effective way, afford to start digitizing the archives.

NBC did already have its own internal production studio centered on repurposing footage and material into new productions. The unit, now known as Peacock Productions, was at the time called NBC News Productions, and was the 2000 brainchild of *Dateline*'s executive producer, Neil Shapiro. One of iCue's top producers, a former producer at Peacock, said of the unit, "We were always very forward-thinking about wringing more dollars out of content that had already been shot. . . . [S]omething like the Mideast peace process . . . *Dateline* and NBC News have covered so much of that situation. We just [go] in the archive, grab that content, repackage it with a story, doing fresh interviews." One of the key people at NBC News Productions was Carol Williams, a longtime veteran of the television news industry. Williams was an award-winning producer of television news and knew the ins and outs of the industry, having worked at many of the major networks as well as cable channels such as Discovery. Steeped in the value and uses of archival material, she was about to help Jones solve his problem.

Fly in the Ointment

As TEA started to ramp up, Chisholm decided it was time to have a go in the corporate world. MIT had begun some collaborations with LeapFrog, an early-childhood learning games and media company that would hire Chisholm away and learn some lessons about edutainment at first hand.

Those LeapFrog-TEA projects centered on what was then LeapFrog's hallmark product, the LeapPad (see the box on LeapFrog). During the collaboration between MIT and LeapFrog, the idea of the Fly, a new product for older children, started to emerge, and Chisholm was hooked. He enjoyed the challenge of trying to figure out new markets. LeapFrog had saturated the early-childhood educational toy space, and it was enthusiastic about new, older markets. Having sought a change from the academic work for some time, Chisholm moved to the West Coast and started work designing the Fly itself, and applications for the Fly.

As with most of LeapFrog's product lines, much of LeapFrog's work involved collaboration with other partners. In the LeapPad line were titles from Disney, Nickelodeon, and more of the usual suspects in children's media. But the Fly was designed for older kids (ages seven to fourteen), and would require new partnerships that not only appealed to their entertainment interests (which they would not want to perceive as being "kidlike"), but also served academic purposes as well.

Although there were many reasons for the lackluster appeal of the Fly, one was the challenge associated with marketing a product that was both fun and educational to an audience outside the early-childhood space.

LeapFrog

LeapFrog is a company founded solely on the success of its educational games and media, albeit for a younger audience. The product that really launched the company was the LeapPad (figure 3.1), which was "paper-based multimedia," a plastic base with an associated stylus into which special books would be inserted. The books had hot spots that could be clicked on with the stylus, eliciting audio responses. For example, a children's book might allow you to click on characters, who would

Figure 3.1
A LeapPad highlighting words to click on.

then say something funny about the action on the page. But it could also be used to quiz readers about things on the page, asking them to click on the word with a long "o," for example.

The LeapPad's primary audience was preschool and early elementary students who were at the prereading to early reading stage. This audience could be skewed up in age through more advanced books, but it was clear that older kids saw the LeapPad as something for younger kids. In some ways, that association of the LeapPad with younger kids was just fine. LeapFrog had made its business selling fun, educational products to preschool and early elementary school–aged students, but it would actually be more accurate to say that LeapFrog had made its business selling those products to the parents of preschool and early elementary school students. The proposition was that these educational products would get kids ready for school by advancing their reading or math skills. The products didn't need to mesh with any set curriculum or provide any accountability; they just needed to have the outward appearance of being educational to parents and fun to kids. The business model was pretty straightforward—market to the parents, who are ultimately the decision makers for purchases for younger kids. Much of the advertising for these products reflects this model, meaning that the typical venue is parent-oriented (or, typically, Mom-oriented) media. In the early 2000s, the model was so successful that it spawned the "green aisle" in toy stores everywhere, indicating to the parents that this was the place to find educational products within the store.

Above eight or nine years old, kids start being turned off by products that are labeled as educational. Furthermore, kids get more of a voice in the purchasing, which means that "Mom" is no longer the purchasing channel for all of the toys. LeapFrog was working on aging up in a number of ways (including videogame platforms such as the Leapster), as well as the Fly (figure 3.2), a pen with an optical

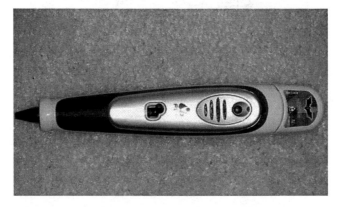

Figure 3.2
The Fly PenTop computer.

reader and special paper (invented by the Swedish company Anoto) that allowed it to read pre-encoded and handwritten marks on the page, aimed at middle school and high school students. Despite the great success that LeapFrog had with the LeapPad, the Leapster, and other handhelds for younger kids, the Fly has struggled, perhaps further evidence of the challenges in the secondary-school-aged educational technology marketplace.

Among the partnerships that were pursued was one with NBC News. Chisholm was instrumental on the LeapFrog side of this discussion. On the other side was Carol Williams.[2] Chisholm and Williams were interested in bringing together educational media and news media so that they could both come alive in a meaningful way for a young audience that often found both news and education irrelevant. Ultimately, the LeapFrog-NBC partnership fell through, and Chisholm later left LeapFrog, though he stayed in touch with Williams. They both remained intrigued by the potential of news media for learning and gestating a different approach to cracking the youth market.

The Next Generation of Educational Media

In the middle of 2005, Williams, knowing of Chisholm's desire to bring together media and games, helped Chisholm connect with the media team gearing up for the 2006 Winter Olympics in Turin Italy, and he jumped at the opportunity. The opportunity to work on online games associated with the Olympics allowed him to further his understanding of the broadcast business while exploring how it would respond to new media. Even while working on the Olympics project, though, neither Chisholm nor Williams let go of their ideas for connecting news media with learning through technology. Chisholm recalls his initial brainstorm:

I remember sitting at home, coming up with this concept [over] the course of a Saturday, where we . . . could take a network's archives and create a social platform where kids could access them and comment and talk about them and use some elements of them for gaming. That was really the beginning of the concept that [I] started thinking about—not just in relation to NBC, but all of the networks and

2. Williams was a key figure in the early stages of iCue, but ultimately disengaged from the project entirely.

where it could go. . . . So really just thinking about all of this stuff that was out there that wasn't being used in education, but that could be, instead of just having everything be boiled down in a textbook.

Initially, despite Chisholm's misgivings about the textbook as an educational medium, they pursued the idea through partnerships with organizations already engaged in the educational space. Textbook publishers were seemingly the ideal candidates for collaboration, as they were (and still are) the primary purveyors of classroom media. In most cases, that medium was (and still is) text. The textbook publishers, however, had increasingly explored, if not embraced, interactive media. Throughout the 1990s, the publishers inserted CD-ROMs in the backs of their books to supplement classroom lessons. As use of the Internet in schools took off in the 2000s, those CD-ROMs were slowly replaced by subscription-based websites that accompanied the textbooks but largely supplied the same sort of supplementary materials that accompanied the textbooks on CD-ROM.

In July 2005, Chisholm and Williams thought up a partnership between NBC News and a textbook publisher; they called it Creating the Next Generation of Educational Media. Their goal was to "create a new set of interactive media for home and classroom use by middle and high school students, leveraging strengths in textbook publishing and NBC's leadership in news." Their plan identified opportunities and challenges in the educational media space for the coming years. In a proposal for the project that was sent to Williams, Chisholm writes about the need and opportunity for a collaboration between NBC News and the textbook publisher:

Over the next five years, as traditional models for educational publishing and testing shift, companies will be forced to explore alternative means of meeting teachers' needs and satisfying adoption requirements in key markets. . . . In fact, many have suggested that textbooks as we currently know them will cease to exist within a decade—this is a somewhat naïve and uninformed perspective that new media eliminate old media; in truth, everything merely converges together in an increasingly complex "media ecosystem." And, while we are still smarting from the sting of previous losses in early CD-ROM and Web-based investments, we must develop new ways of reaching students and develop financial models around new consumer and investor expectations.

As a new starting point, we see a tremendous opportunity to integrate textbooks in AP U.S. History, AP European History, AP World History, and introductory college history courses with Web-based curriculum support materials created with content from NBC News archives. We have a unique opportunity to tie news and current events with textbook content so students develop a better understanding of the causes and effects in history, as well as the interrelationships among events. News clips and broadcast segments would help to put "faces and places" in the minds of students as they work through textbook chapters and exercises. The value of the proposed on-line experiences comes with *self-directed instruction tools that support what they're doing in the classroom, as well as simple games and social learning opportunities to collaborate* with students around the country. (Emphasis added.)

This focus on self-directed learning was the key aspect of the project. The site would capitalize on a social-constructivist format (Vygotsky 1978) for its pedagogical framework, also drawing upon aspects of experiential education (Joplin 1981). The students who constituted the site's community would be able to look through these media archives and make sense of these artifacts and moments of history together, aiming to improve their understanding for their own sakes as well as to do better on the Advanced Placement (AP) exams. In addition to the students mentoring one another and providing feedback on one another's work, there was potentially a role for their teachers to do these things as well. By being confronted with interesting challenges in the form of the site's games, and by challenging one another's assumptions and understandings on the site's forums and comment fields, users would have a rich learning experience radically different from the traditional "top-down" classroom experience that has existed for more than a century.

The Computer Will Blow Up the School

At MIT, any learning technology we explore is done so to some extent in the shadow of Seymour Papert. Papert's legacy is a complex one that has yielded all of the projects in TEA as well as Mitchel Resnick's Scratch group, and of course his own LOGO software, which now has inspired half a dozen extensions. In *Mindstorms* (1980), Papert asserts that the computer "will blow up the school." This idea—that the self-directed learning enabled by computers would at least reconfigure schools and possibly even render schools irrelevant—has been in the mind of every education technologist for decades now.

The idea has some problems, most effectively addressed by Buckingham (2007), but essentially, schools are robust institutions whose practices remain valued by society—often for good reason. Nevertheless, technology is presenting opportunities for change from the static practice through outlets such as games, interconnectivity, and media production. Jenkins was an early observer of these opportunities and codified these new practices in his New Media Literacies group, inspired by the work of Gee (2003), the New London Group (1996), and the like.

As the name suggests, New Media Literacies also points to a set of a new competencies (literacies) that kids should be developing through in-school and out-of-school experiences. These literacies were identified as essential for full participation in twenty-first-century society, and were rarely, if ever, taught in schools. These skills included things such as:

• *Play*—the capacity to experiment with one's surroundings as a form of problem solving

• *Distributed Cognition*—the ability to interact meaningfully with tools that expand mental capacities

• *Collective Intelligence*—the ability to pool knowledge and compare notes with others toward a common goal

• *Judgment*—the ability to evaluate the reliability and credibility of different information sources

• *Transmedia Navigation*—the ability to follow the flow of stories and information across multiple modalities

• *Networking*—the ability to search for, synthesize, and disseminate information

• *Negotiation*—the ability to travel across diverse communities, discerning and respecting multiple perspectives, and grasping and following alternative norms.

In the five years since the debut of this writing and the inception of iCue, Collins and Halverson (2009) and Thomas and Brown (2011) have written excellent treatments of these ideas, highlighting the various capacities and reluctances of schools to embrace new technologically fueled models and the powerful advantages technology can confer. But work has also been done to attempt to seriously understand the culture of youth and technology, both online and off, and many lingering questions remain (Ito et al. 2009; Buckingham 2007; Seiter 2007). Many assert that the gap between the digital haves and the have-nots means that the digital divide is growing wider, not smaller. Some also suggest that the real advantage of working with youth and technology is that you can capitalize on young people's investment in consumer culture to help them develop awareness of mass culture and its practices, both good and bad. Finally, many call into question the ability of all young people to pursue the remarkable self-directed learning that some of them have naturally pursued in affinity spaces and the like. Still, we believe these are arguments in favor of refining our techniques, not abandoning the pursuit of innovative learning practices. And certainly, in 2006, at the inception of iCue, there was no reason not to try.

Chisholm and Williams recognized that each state had its own curriculum standards and frameworks—guidelines that specify the scope of curricula and core ideas in each subject. This diversity presented a challenge in creating a product appropriate for a national scale, so they identified the Advanced Placement market as the next best thing. AP courses are upper-level courses taken by students all over the country. At the end of each course, students typically take a standardized exam (developed by the nonprofit College Board) in the hope of doing well enough to be granted college credit for the course. AP students—academically advanced and motivated—and their parents, given the high stakes of college credit, had already been established as a market with a strong tendency toward spending on supplementary educational materials. The history exams initially chosen seemed like the most straightforward match with the NBC News archives. The top exams in history and English were taken by a total of 700,000 students per year, according to College Board data.

The Coming Revolution in Education

The textbook partnership didn't take off. Conversations persisted for months, but as was usually the case with textbook publishers, the initiative was deemed too risky and too far outside their current models. (Nevertheless, textbook companies would appear regularly throughout the story of iCue.) Given the short deadline on the Olympics project, this new project idled for some time. But once the smoke from the Olympics cleared (or at least once they could see through it), Chisholm and Williams pursued their next-generation approach to educational media fully. At this point, Chisholm became a "utopian entrepreneur" (Laurel 2001) in pursuit of this project, which he thought would create an education revolution in the way history and language were taught. He ultimately would not be the one to lay down the money to make this a reality, but he was the one whose sweat and tears would.

In the spring of 2006, Chisholm focused on these ideas nearly full time, with Williams' support. As a road map for the product he envisioned, he created a scenario called "The Coming Revolution in Education." It played off the simultaneous needs and opportunities in three markets that could come together to benefit one another—education, news, and business. For education, teachers were in need of new, trusted tools that worked with new media, while students were already learning (albeit nonacademic content, outside school) from such media. For news, the market was slipping quickly away from television and to the Internet, especially for young people. As for business, there were many companies looking for a better-trained workforce that was versed in twenty-first-century literacies.

The revolution would be built upon three advances in media and education that Chisholm saw forming the foundation of educational innovations in the coming years:

• *Media convergence*—young people were simultaneously using many kinds of media individually and collaboratively

• *Digital archives*—digital repositories of various media were growing and becoming more prevalent and students were starting to develop skills in using them

• *Games*—young people were playing games online, and the reemergence of educational games as a legitimate field was starting to take place, pointing the way toward innovation in learning games.

The product that was described was firmly focused on the AP courses, for the previously mentioned reasons of national reach and a motivated market. This meant that a direct-to-consumer model could be viable, thereby bypassing the complex purchasing channels of schools. It was also comprehensive, with weekly tie-ins and extensive use of social interactions, video, and games.

Jenkins, meanwhile, had launched a significant project in New Media Literacies (NML), funded by the MacArthur Foundation in 2005. The group's seminal 2006 white paper influenced thinking about games, education, and media everywhere, including internally at MIT. Central to this framework is the notion of participatory culture, in which young people were not merely observers and consumers of media, but rather active participants, through media, in a space inhabited by media and by their peers. Jenkins and his colleagues called out several ways in which that participation is manifest—many of them through games.

Chisholm and Williams's project was a great opportunity to create a product that could not only meet the stated curricular objectives, as had been done with previous TEA games, but also address some of these greatly needed skills for which NML had laid the groundwork. A product that involved games, multiple media, and multiple forms of community participation and discourse was clearly called for by Jenkins's work.

In the first year, the Education Revolution would create three courses—a high-investment course with a lot of materials (AP History), a middle-investment course (AP Government and Politics) with moderate amounts of new materials, and a low-investment course (AP English Literature and Composition) with far fewer materials. These courses had some of the highest subscription levels in the AP market. Total production cost in the first year was estimated at nearly $10 million. But with site subscriptions ranging from $20 to $40, depending on whether the person wanted just video or games and video, it was also estimated that in the first three years it could make revenue of $25 to $40 million, quickly capitalizing on that initial investment. From there, it could grow across subjects and grades.

The Plans for the Revolution

As the product (still known by many names—Clutch, WildFire, JetFuel) moved forward, the plans for how it would start solidified. One of the early product-requirements documents outlined the purpose of the project (called WildFire in this version) internally as:

• Provide access to a vast set of previously unavailable archival materials

• Directly tie archival material to AP course syllabi through browse and search features

• Allow students to explore and play with media through games, blogs, and discussion forums

• Establish a rich "learning community" around the NBC News and partner brands

• Immerse students in a new online educational experience that does not currently exist

It added, "Although we are supporting education through the experience, from the question-of-the-day to the game challenges to the blog assignments, we are not positioning this as 'test prep' or a replacement for classwork. Our design philosophy is that these media work in some relation to the students' overall educational experience, but that we motivate them in different ways through this design." The proposition to its target audience was, "WildFire is a website where you can interact with historical and current events media from [news media] to play games, post blogs, and communicate with friends as you learn what you need to know to do well on AP exams in U.S. History, Government and Politics, and Literature and Composition."

Even in the early phases of design and discussion, games played a prominent role. In order to turn video archives into games, the archives could be transformed into what would come to be called CueCards: discrete media viewers that could be treated as cards as in popular games such as Pokémon, Magic: The Gathering, or even poker. Players would develop their own personal "decks" of stories, collecting historical moments for later use. Discussions of these ideas around the Education Arcade would lead to the thought that these media players could even imitate a contemporary educational tool—flash cards—and be "flippable," with the capacity for storing information and annotations on the back (figure 3.3).

In one of the early documents Chisholm produced for Williams, he describes the idea for a game:

The game's design would encourage players to explore how current events are the direct and indirect results of history. Imagine players trying to reconstitute a series of "dominoes" or sorting through "52 pick up"—each domino or each card represents a [discrete] piece of information from a textbook, archival video clip, or broadcast news clip that players put in order and re-organize. They "play" to assemble relevant bits of information in a cohesive argument or story, constructing and understanding history and current events in new ways that more effectively inform classroom discussion, essay writing, and peer-to-peer communication and

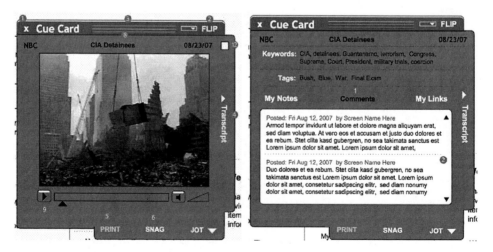

Figure 3.3
The front and back of an early CueCard mockup shows the media player on the front, and the associated data on the back (accessible by "flipping" the player over).

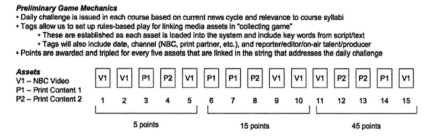

Preliminary Game Mechanics
• Daily challenge is issued in each course based on current news cycle and relevance to course syllabi
• Tags allow us to set up rules-based play for linking media assets in "collecting game"
      • These are established as each asset is loaded into the system and include key words from script/text
         • Tags will also include date, channel (NBC, print partner, etc.), and reporter/editor/on-air talent/producer
• Points are awarded and tripled for every five assets that are linked in the string that addresses the daily challenge

Assets
V1 – NBC Video
P1 – Print Content 1
P2 – Print Content 2

Figure 3.4
The scoring rubric and design for one of the early games. The goal is to connect media in a chain, and players are scored based on tagged links.

collaboration (i.e., role-playing would be key to many of these, as students are "forced" to think about events from perspectives other than their own).

An early design showing a variant of the Dominoes game is shown in figure 3.4. Players are given a starting place (and later an ending place) and asked to make linkages among the media. It is a variant on a typical "six degrees of separation" game associating similar people, movies, and so forth through a chain of intermediaries. Often, in those games, the goal is to make the shortest linkage possible. In the classic "Six Degrees of Kevin Bacon" game, one needs to link Kevin Bacon to other actors by citing films with common costars. So, for example, if one wanted to link Kevin Bacon to Tina Fey, one could find out that Tina Fey was in *Man of the Year* with Audrey Dwyer, who was in *Where the Truth Lies* with Kevin Bacon, giving her a Bacon Number of 2.[3]

In this version of the game, the goal was to make the longest chain possible by connecting the events and ideas represented in the print and video media clips. So, for example, one might try to link a video showing a story featuring a graph of the stock market crash in 2008 and a newspaper headline and story about record unemployment in 2010. One could link those with a couple of intermediate stories about investment banks and business lending—leading to the set of connections where the stock market crash (asset 1) was connected to investment banks (asset 2), which are connected to business lending (asset 3), which is connected to unemployment (asset 4). But others could make longer chains showing intermediate connections to housing markets, lending practices, and the global economy. One could

---

3. Calculated courtesy of the Oracle of Bacon (http://oracleofbacon.org).

even make connections with events in other times and places, linking the stock market crash of 2008 with the crash of 1987, or linking Ben Bernanke to Alan Greenspan. The longer or more interconnected the chain, the more complex and nuanced the understanding of the events required.

This approach was a notable departure from the way that history is often or typically taught. Dominoes represented an innovation. Students could become fluent in history through interpreting cultural and historical narratives, arranging the appropriated narratives of the press into their own stories. Users would essentially be able to remix the past and provide their own spin on the relationships among the events and ideas on the starting and ending cards. Although computerized scoring based on tags provided a first pass on feedback, it was far from being a closed, "guess-what-I'm-thinking" exercise. The game's intent was to be open-ended, with the results evaluated and enjoyed by peers. This allowed students to be creative and innovative, relying on their ability to defend and judge subjective answers, rather than basing answers solely on computerized scoring. Understanding history in this way was much less about teachers explaining stories with names, dates, and places. Instead, it put the students at the center of an activity, trying to make sense of many events across time and space. It challenged them to create their own ideas and knowledge as they interacted with media and their peers. Though teachers were mentioned in the equation, students were the focal point at this stage. Teachers could assign or organize activities, but the activities were entirely student-centered.

This game relied not only on a different way of thinking about history, but also on a complex technical back end. In the form shown in figure 3.5, the linkages would be scored by use of metadata on each of the assets. Assets that shared metadata could be linked, which would require a sophisticated and comprehensive set of metadata. Other versions of the game allowed players to add tags and linkages that they would have to defend and explain to their peers in the community, requiring a means of vetting this information in a manageable way. In the hands of the right media partner, it would all be possible.

It is clear from these initial designs that this was a product targeting students and that it relied on a motivated audience that would be interested in materials related to the students' coursework, but not pushed upon them. There were many ways in which students could interact with the space and its components that leveraged new media and games. The designers figured that students would see the following values in their participation:

• They will get to explore two major media archives (this assumed the participation of the *New York Times,* or another major print news organization, in addition to a television broadcast partner) as they learn important facts, explore ideas, and develop critical-thinking skills essential for AP success;

• It is the only online media and gaming environment that ties news and popular culture to their learning in an ongoing way through the school year;

• It supports their learning *in ways that teachers and textbooks don't* [emphasis added], allowing them to explore new strategies for mastering content and bringing those insights back to the classroom, to their homework, and at the end of the experience to their exams;

• It is the only major learning community designed exclusively to support students taking rigorous and competitive AP courses and exams.

We emphasize that it is leveraging learning, "in ways that teachers and textbooks don't," to show that this wasn't just a new product in concept, but rather a revolutionary educational innovation. This wasn't just a better way to provide what students already had access to through schools and classes; it was a way to directly reach students that capitalized on the online practices with which they were starting to engage.

There were ten basic components to the site in these designs. (A slightly later version, known as "Clutch," is shown in figure 3.5, in this case with an NBC theme.) These were:

1. Home Page

2. Student Profile Page

3. Game Page

4. Blog Page

5. Daily Questions Page

6. Student Center Pages (including Discussion Boards, IM Tools, Creative Media Tools)

7. Course Syllabi

8. Gaming and Creative Palettes

9. Leader Boards

10. Browse and Search (Advanced)

The idea was that the site would be updated frequently (daily for some components and weekly for others) to keep the site fresh. This content would require a lot of work on the part of the production staff but would also provide reasons for the students to come back on a regular basis. At this stage, the game section would be the focus of students' attention, while they could freely go about using the other sections too. They could, of course, connect their work with what was going on in their courses. Teachers would be able to participate as well, to see how students were making connections among the games and the topics in the AP syllabus, and perhaps even to assign participation in the site to the students. This was all

Figure 3.5

An early mockup of a Government and Politics page for Clutch, themed for NBC. A simplified interface continues to show academic, social, and game-oriented components. The titles of "weekly" and "daily" challenges show that the site was designed to be updated and visited frequently. It also shows how student-oriented the design is.

done through the course syllabus, as Chisholm noted, "published from the College Board materials so students can have ready access to the topics and themes on which they will be tested. The syllabi will also provide an easy-access gateway to video assets associated with specific topics so they can browse and review archival material as it relates directly to the syllabi. While not a curriculum, this will allow students and teachers to see how material within the site directly relates to AP subject requirements."

These were exciting ideas that had traction. This vision bore the marks of the work that was previously done at MIT on games and participatory media, so Chisholm was fully supported at home. The question from the MIT side was, "Could a major news network really be attracted to producing an education project?" It would become clear that although there was broad interest from the broadcast news community, NBC News had real reasons to take a major risk, and that it had recently stumbled upon the will to act on those reasons.

Rather than waiting for the industry executives to find TEA and fit it into their dying model, Chisholm now sought to entice them with his new model. Having been through the drill many times before, he made it clear to those in TEA that this time was going to be different. Here was a chance to take the ideas that had been developed at MIT and finally bring them to full scale. Although the frustration of failed collaborations was exhausting, the allure of getting work beyond the ivory tower, out into the field at full scale, was tremendous. The goal of TEA was not just to make games, but to make a difference in the way education is conceived of and delivered.

With Jones in the CFO seat, NBC News was certainly positioned to innovate, or rather to extend the mission of NBC News to a new, logical place. Jones says:

We had our first conversation with the Education Arcade about the concept of iCue, which was very, very exciting. Very experimental, in terms of something its scale. . . . When I presented the idea to the development team, I said this is a very interesting area for us to explore. I think education really lends it naturally to what we do. We are an organization that is geared around informing and educating on a daily basis to our consumer platforms, but our production philosophy is short form. *Nightly News* is basically, you know, nine to ten segments, two to three minutes long. These are sound bytes. But it's not just anecdotally just a snapshot. These stories are written with a beginning, a middle, and an end. Written around, typically the lens of an individual because it makes it far more compelling and therefore it has strong education value. So our production sensibility means that we're probably naturally inclined towards creating educational content.

To confirm the irrelevance of broadcast news to the youth market, early in the process of investigating this new idea, Jones spoke to a test group of AP students, late in their high school careers. Jones describes the experience:

When I got in front of eighteen-year-olds there were a couple of things that were profoundly shocking. The first was that I asked them if any one of them could name any one of the broadcast network anchors [not just NBC], and in that entire room of fifteen to twenty AP students—some of the country's brightest eighteen-year-olds—no one could do it. As a validation of the fact that the traditional side of NBC News was an irrelevant brand to this audience was just . . . it was there in spades, and frighteningly so.

And that was that. Jones did his due diligence, evaluated his risks, and eventually acquired iCue. NBC News was ready to move into a new market—to have a new mission, even if it developed that new mission out of necessity. By embracing participatory culture, it was going to reach out to young people to meet them in their supposedly natural habitat and, it hoped, build an audience of loyal viewers (players? consumers?) for generations to come.

4   Due Diligence

Of course, it's never quite that easy. We left out some details in the previous chapter in order to tell you a story, in part because those details are a story unto themselves. The rights to iCue were not snapped up immediately by NBC; instead, they knocked around between NBC and CBS (and even ABC for a while). Not only were NBC and CBS in competition with each other, but each was trying to guess if it could really pull off such an ambitious project.

After developing the idea initially, Chisholm and Williams had a hard time getting in the door at NBC throughout 2005, despite Williams' connections. Slight variations of the plan for the three major networks were devised (see the designs in figure 4.1), showing the strengths of NBC, ABC, and CBS as the "right" partner to make the project come together. It wasn't until Jones came on board that Chisholm and Williams saw their opening. Chisholm says, "Carol got a meeting with Adam and his team [in June 2006] and very quickly decided to move on it, and think about it. And from NBC's perspective it was, again, really great—education was a great template for thinking about how to digitize this incredible asset they had with the archives."

But executives at CBS got it as well. Chisholm went on a whirlwind tour of the New York news media powerhouses: "Between Tuesday and Friday, I presented the educational media and games deck to the *New York Times*, CBS, NBC, and ABC. It was an absolutely stunning week of 'competition,' providing tremendous insights into the paranoia that drives some of the media business in New York." Though ABC was lukewarm and took a pass, CBS and NBC each asked for exclusive negotiating rights for some time to try to set up the deal. After some thought, Chisholm turned down the exclusive deals in an effort to accelerate the process and "get it done." The

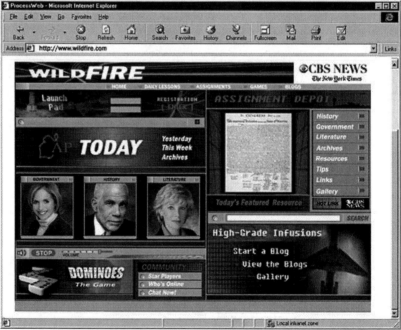

Figure 4.1
Similar designs for the original website, shown with different names (JetFuel for NBC and WildFire for CBS). The sites display content clearly focused on academics (e.g., the Assignment Depot), along with components that were more social (e.g., Blogs) or more game-oriented (e.g., Dominoes).

New York Times seemed interested in working with either network as a partner. Chisholm evaluated a list of pros and cons for the relevant organizations. Katie Couric had just moved from NBC to CBS and could be a good advocate on the CBS side. CBS also had extensive archives, and a separate and quite competent CBS Digital organization. CBS skewed older than NBC, making the project even more important for it, but also a harder proposition. It also wasn't clear where the project would live within CBS, and the existing relationships among Chisholm, Williams, and others with NBC could be compromised if the project were to go to CBS. NBC, on the other hand, was the leading news network, with existing relationships with many of the players. It also had strong anchors and a digital department housed within NBC News. Its online presence was behind the times, though, even on the MSNBC side, and although its archives went back quite a way, older content would have to be licensed for digital distribution.

Negotiations continued. NBC explained that it was working on video support for browsers other than Internet Explorer, including Safari and Firefox. What today would seem like a no-brainer—the need to support other browsers—took a significant effort at the time. But given the education market, an Internet Explorer–only strategy was not possible. CBS execs discussed ways in which they could obtain corporate buy-in and make this a priority. But they wanted assurances of support and sponsorship to spread the financial burden. They were looking for foundations and corporations that might be able to help.

Jones recalls those days as a real contest with his colleagues. The organization saw the K–12 market as being particularly difficult and dominated by textbook companies with much more reach and familiarity with the educational landscape. Beyond that, he was still having difficulty convincing his colleagues that digitizing the archives was even worthwhile. He says:

My response [was], "Well, all of that is true. It is complicated, but that doesn't mean you shouldn't do it. Because if you get back to the first problem, which is if you stay on this course it'd basically be death by a thousand cuts. So we have to change right now, so it's important that we start to experiment in this space. . . . I will show [that] you have to build a business out of nothing with all the problems that we have."

Final presentations and negotiations continued into mid-July. At that time, NBC News was ready to commit, and CBS was still looking for sponsorship. That hesitation left NBC News in the driver's seat and earned it exclusive negotiating rights for three weeks. Although those weeks turned into months, the deal stuck with NBC. What would be known as the NBC iCue ship set sail for waters that were uncharted, at least for a media company. One of the producers looked back at that time:

> I think the uncharted waters analogy, it fits perfectly with Adam. Because no television network had made a decision like that. I'm sure all of them talked about it or wished they could figure out a way to monetize the archives, to be more involved in a growth industry, to figure out a way to get an entire generation of non–TV watchers to at least be familiar with the brand, NBC News. . . . I see NBC News as moving toward all other platforms and not just solely the TV screen. But Adam was the first.

Although the waters that NBC News entered were in many ways uncharted, some may see this (as one producer pointed out in hindsight) situation as a company heading into well-charted waters without the map. As iCue moved toward becoming a reality, we wavered between feelings of being pioneers in new, unexplored spaces and anxiety that all of the "pioneering" was really just following an existing, well-documented trajectory of the new technology that would claim to revolutionize education, but would ultimately be marginalized; such claims had been made for radio, television, film, and other media (Tyack and Cuban 1995). In the end, it seemed that iCue could be on the leading edge of a coming wave in education—private industry, particularly media companies, moving into educational spaces and trying to win the eyeballs of a future market and take a bite out of the educational materials market dominated by the textbook industry, while helping students develop their own self-directed but highly collaborative ways to understand our past and the ways in which we represent it.

Have Any Technologies Been Implemented at Full Scale in Education?

The first thing that becomes apparent as one looks at the history of scaling technology innovations in education is that examples of success are few and far between. If one looks even deeper for examples that more closely parallel iCue—those that would be targeting a secondary-school audience in specific disciplines—the number of examples rapidly approaches zero. (See the box on Other Models and Markets.)

How could that be? Schools are filled with computers and have pushed for Internet connectivity for years through programs such as E-rate to the tune of billions of dollars. Researchers have developed, tested, and advocated for countless new technologies that can make teaching more effective and learning more student-centered. Yet look into the schools of today and you will find little impact of these efforts on day-to-day teaching and learning. Student information systems, PowerPoint presentations, Internet research, and word-processing labs are quite common. But these uses are not transformative in the way many researchers envision educational technology usage. (See the US Department of Education's National Educational Technology Plan 2010.) Look further at most of these technologies and another interesting trend becomes apparent—they weren't originally designed for schools. The use of office tools for writing and presentation or Internet searches for reports reflects business uses brought into schools. Even student information systems, though customized for schools, are really just enterprise databases. The same can be said for the most widespread educational technology, the graphing calculator. There are certainly examples of products that have reached tens or hundreds of thousands of users coming out of academia. We have helped produce some of those products, and there are many others from top-tier researchers around the country. But these are grant-supported projects. They are sustained by continual research investments. When those grants go away, so too will the products they have supported. This situation results in products that are perhaps scalable in reach for some time, but not scalable in terms of their underlying support systems, which rely on continual infusions of grant funds.

Other Models and Markets

Edutainment

So where can we look for examples of technologies that have been brought to full scale in education? It depends on the definition of "scale." If it means ubiquitous use across schools by millions, then this chapter could be wrapped up right here. But there are examples that have increased in scale to some extent across time, in or out of school, that are worth examining. One of the more relevant cases is that not of a product, but of a genre of software—edutainment. We (Klopfer and Osterweil, forthcoming) and others (Ito et al. 2009; Ito 2008; Buckingham 2007) have written about the rise and fall of edutainment software in the 1980s and 1990s. Although the attribution for the decline of this software genre differs slightly, there is an agreement on most of the elements associated with its rise and on many elements of the subsequent fall.

In the early days of personal computers, both at home and at school, there was a strong push for production of software with educational content. Perhaps the pioneer in this space was Oregon Trail, released as part of a collection in 1981 by the Minnesota Educational Computing Corporation (MECC). The Oregon Trail software replayed the lives of early settlers pushing west on the Oregon Trail. Through a series of decisions and (notably) hunting activities, one could learn about the lives and times of these early settlers. The game was (and continues to be—it was rereleased on Facebook in 2011) quite popular. Other titles that proliferated in the 1980s and continue today include the geography game Where in the World Is Carmen Sandiego? and the math game Math Blaster. These games were marketed primarily to consumers, who used them at home on their personal computers, but many schools also purchased copies for the computer labs that were proliferating at the time. Consequently, this software was often used in computer classes at the time or as rewards for students who had finished their regular classwork.

As the CD-ROM took hold in the early 1990s, these titles were updated and expanded. The Living Books series from Broderbund became quite popular. Titles proliferated, and the market rapidly changed. Products that simply promoted "thinking skills" were quickly relegated to the bargain bins in stores everywhere, while titles that tightly targeted readily identifiable academic skills, such as the Jump Start series, became more dominant. These titles promised academic gains for the children of the parents purchasing these products.

Those years were marked by the rapid growth of software companies, which were bought and sold. Perhaps the most interesting story of these is that of the Learning Company. The Learning Company was one of the dominant edutainment companies of the 1990s, publishing titles such as Rocky's Boots and the Reader Rabbit series. The company was founded by three educators, Ann McCormick Piestrup, Leslie Grimm, and Teri Perl, along with game designer Warren Robinett. When the company started in 1979, they were hoping to capitalize on the educational potential of the newly released Apple II computer. The company began with a grant from Apple, but got its real start a couple of years later with a grant from the NSF to develop a product that became Rocky's Boots, a game about logic, circuits, and electrical engineering (Mace and Markoff 1982). Shortly afterward, the company received venture capital funding, and it was off. It later even acquired MECC, the publisher of the Oregon Trail software. The Learning Company went public in 1992.

There ends the simple part of the growth of an educational technology company. In the mid-1990s, when the edutainment era was in its heyday, the company was bought by another company, SoftKey, which later also acquired the other big name in edutainment of the era, Broderbund. This sale was later followed by Mattel purchasing all of the companies for nearly $4 billion in 1999, only to be sold off years later to a holding company for pennies on the dollar (Cave 2000). The story continued into the 2000s, when Riverdeep, an interactive software company, acquired both the Learning Company and Broderbund and capped off its acquisition with the purchase of the textbook publisher Houghton Mifflin Harcourt.

Given all of these purchases, it is hard to ascribe value or impact to any single company in this mix. Together, they made up almost every player of the edutainment era. Collectively, it seems to be a story of products designed for the education market going to a larger scale. Individual titles within these collections have sold millions or even tens of millions of copies across the years. NBC certainly had some things to learn from this era—both models to emulate and those to avoid. On the plus side, this era showed that products could be marketed to homes and schools and still sell millions of copies. However, there are many caveats in that positive lesson. First, with few exceptions these products were designed for elementary school, or perhaps middle school. There was little to no market for high school products of this ilk. Second, the products were rarely integrated into curricula, but instead used as part of computer classes or enrichment activities, marginalizing much of this work. Perhaps most importantly, though, the rise of the Internet killed off the market for these products almost entirely, never to be resurrected. Once schools got their hands on free resources via the Internet, there was no need to pay for and manage software licenses for supplementary products. The home market followed along similarly, essentially ending the CD-ROM era.

The Secondary-School Market

The secondary-school market, the one that NBC News was aiming for with iCue, has conspicuously few stories to tell about increasing the scale of educational technologies. That isn't to say that there are no such stories. Most textbooks come with online problem sets and homework support. Intelligent tutors, such as those offered by Carnegie Learning, are also quite popular. These systems provide dynamic, customized feedback to students as they work through problems, particularly in domains that have clear parameters, such as mathematics. Tutors can either be integrated with whole curricula from the providers, including textbooks, or added as supplements to traditional texts. Either way, although these systems do provide a student-centered learning opportunity, they don't fundamentally change

what or how students learn. Examples that are both successful and transformative in this way are even harder to find.

One that has succeeded for quite a few years is Geometer's Sketchpad
(K.C.P. Technologies 2009). Designed in the 1980s as part of a National
Science Foundation–funded project, it came to market in 1991 as a product
delivered by Key Curriculum Press. Geometer's Sketchpad is notable not
only for its long-lived success, but also because it really pushed pedagogy.
It provided a way of graphically and interactively working with equations
and mathematical concepts. Though designed originally for geometry, it
has been applied in algebra, trigonometry, and calculus throughout the
high school curriculum. Through the use of the graphical interface, Geometer's Sketchpad is designed to be used directly by students, but it can also
serve as a means for teachers to illustrate concepts quickly and easily at
the front of the room. As with any such technology, when the change in
pedagogy can be marginalized it usually is, and many use cases are quite
teacher-centric. Today, Geometer's Sketchpad is still in use and has a Web-
delivered version. But it may be a case of too little too late. The company
is struggling to stay alive in this era of slim school budgets and other free
tools (Steven Rasmussen, cofounder of Key Curriculum Press, personal
communication, December 2010).

Another example that reached into the secondary-school market is
SimCalc. Roschelle, Tatar, and Kaput (2008) offer a compelling history of
the product from concept through research and scaling. SimCalc was the
brainchild of Jim Kaput, a professor at the University of Massachusetts,
Boston. The product was envisioned by Kaput in the late 1980s and early
1990s as a means to transform mathematics teaching and learning and a
way to capitalize on the benefits of computation for classroom learning.
As with Geometer's Sketchpad, a NSF grant kicked off this project in the
mid-1990s. The technology was incredibly expensive to develop on a per-
student basis, at an estimated $10,000 per student in the early days of
testing. That cost is to be expected of a research project. As the project
progressed over the years, the product and process changed as a result of
feedback from research. Professional development materials and curricula
supported the use of the software. By Roschelle, Tatar, and Kaput's (2008)
account, by the year 2000 they were starting to think about scaling up;
they read up on the process, further specified their innovation, and thought
about partners. By the mid-2000s, they were conducting some scale-up

experiments, with the most significant scale-up coming in what they describe as the sixth phase of the project, from 2005 to 2008. They describe the results of those experiments as encouraging and as a potential precursor to additional scale-up experiments.

The details of this story reflect the careful thought involved in the design, implementation, and research required to sustain and enlarge the scale of this product. But they also reflect a journey that took nearly twenty years—which amounts to something like ten to twenty times as long as most companies would bear for scaling up. And the process is not even done yet. So, although this story of scaling up provides a lot to learn from, it in many ways clearly illustrates the disconnect between the worlds of academia and industry.

Previous Media Ventures

The iCue project wasn't the first time media companies ventured into education. For years, news media have made resources available to enable teachers to gather discussion materials quickly for "current events" in social studies and history classes. This approach can be seen today on many of the news networks sites. For example, Turner Broadcasting and its major news network, CNN, have produced materials for students and teachers, initially through Turner Learning and then directly through CNN. But there have been attempts that were more significant over the years. In some cases, these ventures have involved the creation of materials or services for schools and teachers. The AOL@School venture around the year 2000 was one such initiative. On the surface, it was an easy on-ramp for schools to the Internet (just as it was for homes at the time). Although it was provided as an educational service, it was often criticized for being nothing more than a marketing scheme and another way to reach customers. The short-lived service attempted to provide student and teacher materials along with professional development services, but met with little success.

There have been some notable forays by the news media into education through acquisitions. Most notable among these was the *Washington Post*'s acquisition of the Kaplan testing service in 1984. With declining newspaper revenues, as of this writing the Kaplan division of the *Washington Post* accounts for more than half of the revenue of the entire company, through its testing service and online higher education business. Though this may have sustained the *Post*, the two entities have sometimes made unusual bedfellows, as Kaplan's practices within the higher education space have come into question, leaving the *Washington Post* in a bind about how to report on these issues.

Another high-profile acquisition came post-iCue in 2010. Rupert Murdoch's News Corp. purchased Wireless Generation, a provider of educational software and services. Not coincidentally, this acquisition happened shortly after Joel Klein, former chancellor of the New York City schools, was appointed executive vice president of News Corp. During this acquisition, Murdoch released a statement saying, "When it comes to K through 12 education, we see a $500 billion sector in the U.S. alone that is waiting desperately to be transformed by big breakthroughs that extend the reach of great teaching" (News Corporation 2010). That's exactly the same kind of thinking that got NBC News into the business.

Before leaving the discussion of media company forays into the world of education, it is worth mentioning the Apple Classrooms of Tomorrow (ACOT) program as a significantly backed attempt to change schools through media. Although the Apple Computer of 1985, when ACOT started, may not have been a media company, Apple, Inc., as of this writing, as ACOT[3] is under way, most certainly is. The ACOT program started in the mid-1980s as a demonstration and research project pushing the boundaries of computer use in classrooms. It focused on transformative practices, in-depth research, and professional development. The ACOT program was run by Apple as a corporate partner, but it wasn't designed to be a direct pathway to profitability. Instead, it was a way of understanding how computers could really transform teaching and learning, perhaps with the hope that such transformation would lead to better products and a larger market in the future. As such, one of the things ACOT tried to understand was how it could get innovations to spread from one classroom or school to another. It turned out that this problem is quite complex. As the Apple Computer of the mid-1990s struggled, ACOT was dismantled after ten years and countless studies conducted by Apple, only to return in the mid-2000s as a project much more tightly focused on high school learning and retention. Perhaps one of the more notable outcomes from these studies is that increasing the scale and diffusion of educational innovations relies as much on context as on the product itself.

The Innovation of iCue

Before we delve into the details of why iCue was invented, what purpose it served, what it actually was, and what it became, we'd like to set the stage for these questions in the context of these previous efforts to increase the scale of innovations. The main question is, "Why would iCue be any different?" We've discussed previous products from the edutainment era, as well as serious academic initiatives. But what set iCue apart? And why is this important as we look forward?

Resources—When looking at most of the past initiatives and how they increased in scale (or didn't), it is clear that they were operating on focused, limited budgets. Whether they received seed money or grant money, most of these products had limited resources available to them. Although the extent of the resources that were drawn upon for iCue may not have been obvious from the start, it was clear that the increase in scale could be significant.

Time—Although financial resources were plentiful, time was not. iCue was part of a profit center at a commercial organization. It could invest resources, but it needed to turn those resources into tangible profits in short order. It could not take decades, in the manner of SimCalc. It needed to happen in months.

Assets—iCue was built on the plentiful media assets that news organizations were sitting on. This would give iCue a potentially large relative advantage if those assets could be used effectively.

Communications—NBC News sat in a position of power with great (albeit shrunken and declining) reach. It did not need to rely on word of mouth to promote a new product. It could broadcast the news about iCue far and wide.

Partnerships—NBC News knew from the start that it didn't want to go it alone on the venture of iCue. But it had a large network based on past collaborations and corporate reach that could allow it to draw upon or create partnerships in a wide variety of areas.

Innovation—Although many of the products emerging from academia were and remain innovative, the same cannot be said for past attempts in the commercial sector, particularly media. AOL@School was not an innovation that demanded change. The current events outreach from news organizations does not involve great innovation. For better or worse, the design of iCue dictated a change in the way that people used it to learn.

These factors both differentiate iCue's story from previous stories of innovation in education and foretell new ones. Others are sure to follow on the path that NBC News has taken. Educational innovation is a space of great need, and technologies present great opportunity. Companies in many sectors, particularly media, are seeing these opportunities and starting to act upon them. The lessons here can, we hope, inform them.

5 The Skunkworks

From: Carol Williams
Subject: February 15 Deadline
Date: Wednesday, November 22, 2006, at 3:31 p.m.
To: iCue Production Team

Just came from a lunch meeting. It is imperative that we meet the February 15 [2007] deadline. The news division is willing to allocate additional resources within reason to make this date. . . . I know this seems like a gargantuan and overwhelming endeavor, but breaking it into manageable sections will help us get a handle on it, and if any group can make it happen, this one can. I have the utmost confidence in all of you. From now until delivery we're in modified crash mode. Please don't hesitate to ask for what you need.

—Carol Williams, in an email to her iCue lieutenants

What we need is February 15, 2009, to be the deadline.

—iCue staffer, in response

Believers

NBC acquired iCue late in the summer of 2006, and by the winter of 2006–2007, approximately sixty producers were working on iCue. The project grew quickly because the deadline for the massive project was exceptionally short, as seen in the previous memo. A force this size was unwieldy, but necessary given the task ahead. Fortunately, this project— almost certainly due to its educational nature— attracted *believers*. Each of the people working in high-level positions on iCue would be dedicated and driven from the start—people who believed in journalism and its responsibilities and in the power of archival media for learning.

The entire production staff for iCue was stashed away in a disused studio in 30 Rockefeller Plaza, Studio 3B. This placement kept a huge staff increase for a new project out of the daily view of many other residents, who were part of a shrinking business and whose jobs were on the line. Studio 3B was typically used for election coverage, but would be unused for at least a year and a half, making it the perfect place to hide this enterprise while meeting the tight deadline. Temporary workstations were set up, and over the course of that fall, more and more producers were crammed into the space. At the same time, MSNBC was moving in to share space with the *Nightly News* group across the hall. Absent the cameras, though, the rooms looked remarkably similar in terms of the crowds. Producers were grouped into their topic areas—US history, US government and politics, and English language and composition (literature having been pared away)—coordinating the digitization of the news pieces, matching them to the Advanced Placement curriculum, and beginning to imagine what the fully implemented version of the project could look like.

The Team

At the top was Carol Williams, in the role of executive producer. Under her was Soraya Gage as senior producer, taking on management tasks for the entire team in addition to managing the US history section. Gage had started at NBC as a page after college and moved through the news industry with great ambition, working all over the world, helping start international branches of the *Christian Science Monitor*'s television network, and ultimately producing Tom Brokaw's long-form documentary pieces for *Dateline NBC* right before moving to iCue (in addition to helping Williams with some long-form features for NBC News Productions). Although many thought she was crazy to leave the Brokaw position when Williams asked her to come on board at iCue, Gage was excited about the new challenge:

I loved the idea that the archives were going to be seen again because I did really value the archives. When I looked at all of that tape . . . I learned so much that I didn't know. We watch the news every night and it passes and it's interesting, and you're kind of paying attention to it but not that deeply. But if you go back and look at it, a lot of thought went into those pieces. . . . I loved the whole civil rights coverage, the Native American coverage . . . there are real treasures in the archives. I was really excited to bring that to light.

I also just felt that I would be doing a service . . . it felt meaningful to me. I loved the idea that it was using technology because kids use technology. I thought it was tapping into a lot of really relevant things—the social networking, the gaming, the use of the archives. I loved the [Cue]card itself—the functionality of it was really cool. . . . I didn't see then but I see now that it really could become a custom digital textbook.

Gage was not Williams's only pull from the NBC News Productions family, either. Mark Miano was hired to run the US government and politics division, based mostly in Washington, DC. He was working in NBC News Productions' offices in Burbank, California, when he was offered the iCue job. Miano considers himself a storyteller by trade and was tired of working on documentaries for topics such as "Dog, the Bounty Hunter." In iCue, he found a way to use archival media as a real source for learning:

Whenever we showed off iCue or . . . archival content to teachers, there's this visceral reaction that they have that's very similar to what I think a journalist has when they see these old stories. I had this "aha" moment maybe six months to a year into the project. I was screening all this content that the team was finding and . . . aligning to the Government and Politics course, and I screened this story that I am convinced was the first news story I ever saw as a kid. . . . Nixon resigned from office, and it's the famous day where he gives his speech to his staff, he boards the helicopter and turns around. I was a kid and I was playing on the floor in my dad's bedroom, and the TV was on and he was watching the news, and all of a sudden he said to me—he goes, "Watch this. This is really important. Watch this." . . . So . . . I'm in my office screening . . . that broadcast again and it was incredible because first of all there was that connection to my childhood, but also I realize when I saw the story anew how much richer it was in terms of—Nixon wasn't this cardboard character, just turning around in the helicopter. He gave this incredibly moving speech to his staff without notes. We went back after I saw this, and we pulled just the raw of the speech, and it's incredible. He's overwhelmed with sadness. And Brokaw's report on this is incredible, but he says at one point in the story something along the lines of, "One can't know the highest mountains unless you've been in the deepest valleys." It just resonated with me because Nixon became this three-dimensional person. It wasn't this cardboard—"I am not a crook." It was a real person who was going through the biggest trial of his life, or any president's life probably. So that, to me, was the "aha" moment.

If I write about Nixon's resignation, it may be a very well-told story in the textbook, but it's just different to see him choked for words. It's different to see him surrounded by his daughters who are teared up, to see the shots of his staff listening to this, and Kissinger crying in the crowd. It just conveys it in a way—and that's why I talk about that visceral reaction when you see the content. I've read a lot of textbooks [while] preparing the outlines for mapping our content, but nothing can quite match actually seeing it—seeing it and hearing it the way it was that night. I have a lot of examples of stuff like that, of old stories that we found or raw footage. It's just amazing that iCue did that.

Beth Nissen rounded out the subject-area leaders, heading up English language and composition. Nissen was an extremely experienced journalist and producer, having worked at the *Wall Street Journal* and *Newsweek*, and then *ABC World News Tonight* and *Nightline* before experimenting with online journalism at CNN.com. When the dotcom boom fizzled, she went back to TV, working at CNN, WGBH, PBS, *Nova*, and Nova ScienceNOW before coming to iCue. She also taught journalism in Columbia University's journalism program, where she had gotten her start. She says:

But the job at NBC, working for iCue, promised to link all of those things. To link my interest in good writing, in language arts. Link my knowledge of and experience in science. Pull it all into the realm of teaching. This is why I became a journalist; [it] was to—in the over-used [phrase], now on coffee mugs—Gandhi saying, "You must be the change you wish to see in the world." I wanted to see a world that functioned better and made smarter decisions and was more tolerant. The way to get at all of those things is through education, is through information. It struck me as early as 1995 but especially after 2000—the last ten years—that the information age is a misnomer. It's really a data age. There's a huge difference between data and information. The amount of information that's actually processed and fact-checked and put into context is minuscule compared to the volume of data and putative or alleged information. So this was perfect for me because it allowed me to do this using the tools of the twenty-first century and for an audience that is important and growing and is not completely shaped yet.

The distinction between data and information captured what NBC News was trying to do with iCue, in contrast to what was currently available. There was (and is) a lot of data available on the Internet, and for the most part that wasn't particularly useful to teachers or decipherable by students. Instead, iCue was an attempt to put information at the fingertips of learners and help the students make sense of that information on their own. It was helping them *really* enter the information age, something that schools have been accused of not doing well.

Wrestling the Archives

Even though there was clear value in the archives, those first months were stressful. Early investigations of the process of turning these historic and important news stories into the dynamic interactive media objects wanted by the NBC News team revealed a huge number of problems.

First, there was simply the issue of finding material. The archives were (mostly) stored in a warehouse in New Jersey, and over the course of eighty years, the tape-logging standards had been inconsistent, to say the least. Producers would have to look through spotty record logs to find material that corresponded with the curricula that were being developed. Once the appropriate tapes were found, producers would have to watch each tape in its entirety and try to determine what material would be relevant in the classroom and how the material could be shaped into Internet-ready segments of five minutes or less.

Second, there was the question of what materials could be used. A great majority of the news reports being sorted and prepared for distribution through iCue had materials in them from agencies such as the Associated Press, Corbis, and Getty that had all been cleared for their original use—a single broadcast—and nothing more. Long before the days of the Internet, current distribution channels could hardly have been anticipated. Interviewees and, in many cases, the estates of interviewees had to be sought out in order to clear the rights to those interviews. Jones understood that although these costs would be massive in the near term, there would be major benefits in the long term, and decided to clear all of the rights to everything he could, in perpetuity and for download.

There was also the issue of vetting and contextualizing the content. The NBC News product, though of high quality, was not necessarily a ready-made product for the classroom. Producers had to create a new set of standards, more stringent than broadcast standards, and vet every asset. Clips were screened for, among other things, profanity, sexuality, and violence. Some stories also required additional context, so staff members were set to work on creating "wrappers"—introductions to the news stories. Other staffers would have to go back to add chirons (the graphics at the bottom of the screen, which can be used to identify the speaker or location on screen), because no student was going to know who long-retired NBC anchors and reporters were, or the once-known-but-now-likely-forgotten figures in the pieces.

Related to this was the massive issue of metadata. Each CueCard had a place for users to put their own tags on the card, but the cards also had a series of keywords that would be used for filtering and searching for material and to provide the spine for the game play. The Dominoes game for which Chisholm had developed the concept while selling iCue had come to be known as Connections. In order for that game to work, the CueCards had to measure the relative strength of those connections by checking the number of keywords that the connected CueCards had in common. Producers quickly became overwhelmed as they tried to determine the appropriate metadata and metadata standards for the CueCards. If John F. Kennedy appears in a clip, what does the clip receive for a keyword? John F. Kennedy? President Kennedy? President John F. Kennedy? JFK? When developing metadata for thousands of assets over hundreds of topics while trying to keep the assets available to all three planned courses, the task was more than daunting—it was maddening.

Finally, each course had its own unique challenges as well in matching news stories to the curriculum of its AP topic. For instance, Gage realized that she and her team would have a hefty gap of US history to fill before the advent of their archival news media:

I realized in U.S. History that the first 450 years were missing. All the history courses started in 1450 and the archives started in 1920. I had to figure out how we fill the gaps. So I worked closely with this teacher, and we identified how many pieces we had to do and then we identified experts who could cover as many of those subjects as possible. On any given day, we interviewed five professors . . . across maybe thirty, forty subjects . . . and then [the AP teacher and the editorial team] wrote the scripts. Then we went to the Library of Congress National Archives and found illustrations.

I said, "They're gonna be about two minutes long. They're only going to deal with one concept; so if it's mercantilism, it's mercantilism. It's not anything else. It has to be an engaging first paragraph to draw the reader, viewer in. And then the last paragraph has to tee it up in the pantheon of history. So if you ever looked at them all together, you would have a complete record of history." And that was kind of the formula.

Beth Nissen ran into other—and, in many ways, thornier—problems in preparing stories for English Language and Composition. Although the AP courses for US History and US Government and Politics had preexisting outlines, there was not one for English. The College Board provides some paragraphs on what the students should be able to do on the exam and a list of suggested authors for the students to study, but it doesn't even provide a list of suggested works. Nissen was significantly helped by a long-existing affinity space, part of her iCue audience:

I got on some AP listservs [email lists], some AP English listservs, and I spent a couple of weeks going through them and watching for panic notes dating back to August along the lines of "Hi, please, I need help. . . . They just asked me to teach AP English language composition. I'm thrilled, but I just realized there's no course outline and classes start in three weeks. Can someone help me?"

Teachers are so generous. They would post their outlines. I ended up collecting about two hundred of these course outlines and then winnowed them down to fifteen that I thought were the most complete and the most surprising—in a way, creative or innovative. I spent Thanksgiving weekend, starting on Thanksgiving Day—I spread them out around my apartment and I walked around in circles all day and took bits and pieces from the best and made what is now the language arts outline.

Her outline assembled, Nissen could then focus on another problem—matching the archives to this outline. She too found that her subject area was not particularly well matched to the archive. It was not a simple matter of pulling in appropriate media, but rather thinking about the media in new ways. For a language arts curriculum, she could highlight clips featuring favorite authors and expose the writing that had gone into producing a segment by highlighting scripts and transcripts. She could pull writing samples from the archives of iCue's partners the *New York Times* and the *Washington Post*. She also took on the media literacy component, preparing content about the "reading" of graphs, maps, and photographs. But there were segments of the curriculum demanding that iCue become an engine yet again for new content, not just archival content. For instance, Nissen and her team created elaborate animations clarifying the Latin and Greek roots of vocabulary words.

This was a clever solution to a gap in the archives, but the more the producers had to create these new clips, the more their resources were drained and the further they were from their strengths. This extra effort was substantial. Some of it reflected the unforeseen constraints of developing material for delivery to the classroom; other parts were simply the challenges of bringing twentieth-century media into the hands of twenty-first-century kids. These problems were unforeseen by Jones and his team during the rapid lead-up to the project, and it cost the project a great deal of money; rights clearance, metadata, gaps in the archives, mismatches in the archives, editing for a new audience—the list goes on. With a longer timeline, the project might have been able to foresee these issues, but in seizing the moment (which would prove key), there was no time for such analysis. The number of hours poured into researching the archives and the metadata, combined with the hours hunting down clearances, combined with the costs of those sweeping clearances, incurred a massive cost for the project. Certainly, having those resources cleared in perpetuity and having metadata standards developed for an online archive would be useful to NBC as a whole over time, but the fact was that iCue was going to be stuck with the bill.

Initial Designs

Meanwhile, aside from the group working on the archival content and curriculum, a team was working hard to get the project made. Before a line of code could be written for the site, there was a great deal to do. To develop a clear vision of what the site was and could be, the team developed a thorough business requirements document that mapped out the site's specifications and also developed a Flash demo in order to communicate the site's value quickly and effectively to everyone from new employees and research staff members to potential partners. The initial designs clearly targeted students as the consumers of the product, though the mechanism through which it would reach those students was yet to be determined. It might be direct-to-consumer or delivered through schools. Preparing for the latter case, there was mention of teacher components in the business requirements document, although they were not highlighted.

Producer Kathy Abbott and Chisholm managed the development process for the demo. The five-screen demo was heavily themed with NBC's corporate branding and contained recent footage from *NBC Nightly News*, and one particularly crucial element— proof-of-concept that iCue's central feature, the CueCard, was working. Cards could appear and play video, but they were able only to suggest some of the CueCards' more innovative features such as flipping or accepting tags and annotations. (See figures 5.1 and 5.2.)

The Connections game (formerly called Dominoes) was also implemented as a purely demonstrative version—it had no real game functionality, but was enough to communicate the idea (see figure 5.3). It was impossible actually to play the game, but viewers could get a sense of the game's functionality. Players watch the first video, then the second. They then "search" through the site's "archives" to find CueCards they might use to connect the two stories.

The real site, however, was not going to be built so quickly. The iCue team brought on a young information technology specialist who had been

Figure 5.1
iCue's appearance on October 24, 2006. Note the appearance of several potential partners in addition to rampant NBC Peacock theming—MIT, the College Board, the *New York Times*, the *Washington Post*, and Intel.

working with General Electric for six years, with a more recent focus at NBC, to begin figuring out what needed to be built. The specialist, Michael Levin, was asked to create a business requirements document for iCue in November/December 2006 from the implications of the demo and from interviews and collaboration with Chisholm and Abbott. He had to act quickly as well, if iCue were to launch in February 2007.

I had a pretty bullish boss at the time, so he thought anything was possible and was like, "Sure, Adam, we'll build anything you want by February." So I actually spent the entire Christmas break, that entire two or three weeks, here in the office with Kathy and Alex—just all day. It seemed like forever to get those requirements

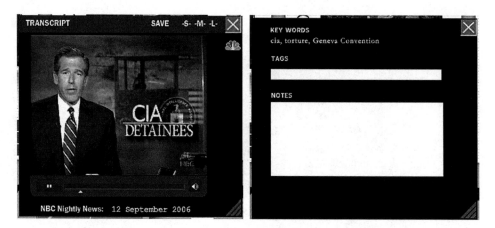

Figure 5.2
The same October 24, 2006, build. The CueCards were simply implemented, able to be flipped, tagged, annotated, and outfitted with a small (!) set of keywords. The "Transcript" button was not yet functional.

built out in such a way that we could actually take the next step to get this thing built up by February.

Obviously, we never launched in February.

The document ended up being a ninety-page behemoth that would describe a product significantly different from the iCue that was released in 2008. (As Levin notes, iCue wasn't released in February 2007.) Levin relates, "There were a lot of other pieces to it because we had initially conceived iCue as having a consumer side and an institutional side. eCommerce was part of it as well, to facilitate the subscription transactions. It was pretty full. What iCue is today [in 2010] is maybe 75 percent or 80 percent of what the original business requirement was going to be." This lack of clarity about the market for iCue would prove a problem that iCue would face over the course of its development (discussed in further detail in chapter 6). Would the product be self-sustaining based on a direct-to-consumer model, or would the product need to be sold to districts, schools, and teachers?

Digital Design Squads

In an attempt to answer that question, although the NBC News team was immersed in production, the Education Arcade's team began to implement

Figure 5.3
The demo's depiction of the Connections game. Although the stories of Florida in the 2000 election and Ohio in the 2004 election didn't take a lot of imagination to connect, the game allowed viewers to see how news stories might be connected.

what came to be called Digital Design Squads in three East Coast cities: Boston, New York City, and Washington, DC. The squads were composed of high school AP students and teachers in the relevant content disciplines: US history, US government and politics, and English language and composition. Using their lens as media investigators, the Education Arcade researchers wanted to know what the media lives of the students were like and how this related to the adoption of iCue—something like a traditional focus test. Over the course of the 2006–2007 school year, these students would provide MIT and NBC News with important baseline information about the media diet of these young people, their interest in online educational media products, and, ultimately, early prototypes of iCue.

Although the target audience's expertise came to bear in many different ways, such as sharing some of the audience's favorite online media sites and commenting on potential designs for the look and feel of the site, there were a few key takeaways.

First, these driven students were mostly interested in the site if they thought it would help them improve their scores on the AP tests. Although they enjoyed the subject matter, they were not necessarily interested in using such a site in their spare time unless it was directly connected to improving their performance on the AP tests. Interest in the product was pretty solid, and many students really liked it. They often struggled with how to describe the site, perhaps because of the new approach it took, unlike other sites in which they participated. Some students described it "like a video game, but not," or a "website that helps with schoolwork, but more interesting." One of the teachers described it to her colleagues as "sort of a game, a Web community, where students could get incentives to learn." Although some students were fine with the inability to describe the site, others said that they didn't get the point. One student asked, "Was it to help with schoolwork? Prepare them for the exam? Review what they'd be learning in class?" It was clear that although the product had a potential niche to fill, it would need messaging about where it fit in the educational experience.

Second, although they were (unsurprisingly) interested in social networks, the students were surprisingly much more excited about the advent of Facebook than they were about MySpace. Perhaps ironically from today's perspective, the privacy protections of Facebook in 2006 were preferable to those of MySpace, which essentially had none; this was potentially valuable information for the design of iCue. This pattern would also be borne out in danah boyd's research into the topic, in which the driven, college-bound students preferred Facebook, whereas the teens who felt marginalized stuck to MySpace (boyd 2007).

At the time, the scope of social networking sites was pretty narrow. They were for posting status updates and pictures and linking to friends. They weren't sites where you played games, took quizzes, or "friended" companies, and they occupied a small piece of teens' online time. Perhaps reflecting that isolated purpose, students were somewhat apprehensive about connecting their accounts on the rapidly ascendant Facebook to iCue. When that potential connection was mentioned after Facebook flirted with incorporating iCue, one student said, "There is no way I'd get any work done." And others echoed the idea that connecting with Facebook would take away from the learning focus of the site. They also wanted to be sure that their profiles within Facebook would be separate from the ones within iCue, so that their "pictures from Facebook couldn't wind up in iCue." Both students and teachers were worried about the content filtering done at schools that block Facebook and other social networking sites, which could affect the ability to use the site within schools. Still, students wanted to make sure there would be an "About Me" profile-style section in any version of iCue. This wish was in direct opposition to the wishes of teachers, who wanted to make sure there would be only the most minimal identifying information about their students on the site. This issue highlights some of the tensions the team was bound to navigate as it determined the market for the site and its feature set.

Finally, the students filled out a media diary over the course of an average week, tracking the details of their media lives. What the results of those diaries conveyed (as displayed below in figures 5.4 and 5.5) was that these successful, ambitious students were shut out from their use of media during

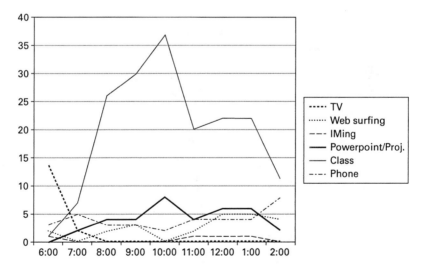

Figure 5.4
The Daytime media use of our Digital Design Squad students (*n* = 45). Class time occupies most of their days between 9:00 a.m. and 3:00 p.m., with music being turned off just before school and quickly coming on after school. PowerPoint does remain a medium supported in schools at a constant, albeit low, level.

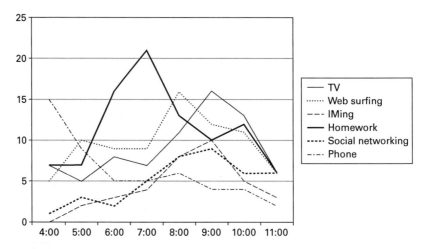

Figure 5.5
The evening media use of our Digital Design Squad students (*n* = 45). The use of many media throughout the evening hours is quite apparent. Although homework between the hours of 6:00 p.m. and 8:00 p.m. drives some of the other media down in that time, web surfing, instant messaging, and music remain fairly high across the after-school hours.

the school day. The most prevalent media they encountered during the day was PowerPoint, frequently the simplest media-authoring tool for teachers to master and thereby "address" local technology standards. At night, however, these students became master multitaskers, fitting homework in among the use of such diverse media technologies as the phone (texting included), social networking, and television. This drove iCue producers to conclude that there was room to innovate in the classroom, and a demand for media outside the classroom. They wanted to get to both of those places quickly.

The media diaries clearly illustrated that during the day, students were engaged in activities that lacked both media and social interaction. On their own time, although they were still doing homework, their lives were filled with media and social interaction. At this point, iCue was still being developed with the idea that it would be purchased by schools *or* by individuals to use at home, but these vastly different patterns cast these two worlds in stark relief. Although it had the potential to bridge a wide chasm, it also had the potential to fall right into that chasm. According to a 2009 report from the National Center for Education Statistics (Gray, Thomas, and Lewis 2010), even a couple of years later, the educational technology practices in which students are engaged in schools are relatively mundane. Although 61 percent of teachers have students "sometimes or often" write on computers, 69 percent have students practice basic skills, and 66 percent facilitate research on computers, only 9 percent have students contribute to blogs and wikis, and 7 percent participate in social networks. Even conducting experiments on computers or making movies or webcasts on computers is done in only 25 percent of the classrooms surveyed. Creative, constructive, participatory activities are mostly missing in the space of school, even when students outside schools are engaging at higher levels in these activities (albeit clearly less than 100 percent).

Among these students, most were happy with the idea of using iCue on their own time, though they didn't necessarily see it as something that they would *purchase*. Students were happier about an institutional purchase of the product than a personal one, and teachers found that to be a reasonable model. What was less clear was what the fallout from the institutional purchase model might be in terms of personalization, networking, and the freedom to explore and participate. One teacher was confused about the activities and time structure and said that she wanted to be able to keep her kids at the same pace and see who might be lagging behind in the activities. This view, which reflects the standard teacher-centered paradigm of many classrooms, would ultimately be a huge challenge for the positioning of iCue. The institutional purchasing model, though appealing to kids, would obviously be less appealing to schools, which would have to find the funding for the purchase and navigate the waters of student use outside the school walls in terms of access, privacy, and protection.

It is also notable what teachers didn't say. Within the education research community, it is believed that what is needed to effect change in schools is more research—credible evidence that particular methodologies or tools produce measurable change. Although the demand for such evidence-based practices may be (and perhaps should be) increasing, there was no evidence that this was one of the barriers that iCue faced. In the Digital Design Squads, teachers did not demand such evidence, but rather acclimated to the activities they saw with their own practices and that went where they wanted their students to go. The practices may not have mapped one-to-one with improvement on a test, but the teachers seemed to feel that the kinds of activities in iCue in which kids would be engaged resonated with the kinds of activities they thought would build the skills they wanted their students to have. Some of those skills would have obvious consequences on the AP exam (e.g., writing the essay questions); others perhaps just seemed like good habits of mind that would work well in that context (e.g., discussion with peers).

Defense

Jones, meanwhile, had somewhat adopted the persona of the corporate gunfighter or Mafioso (his cell-phone ringtone is the theme from *The Godfather*) and was busy defending his secret "skunkworks" project, protecting it from scrutiny as it hemorrhaged money, digitizing the archives, clearing the rights, and getting the archives iCue-ready. He repeatedly had to go to the plate for the project with his corporate superiors:

Within three months of starting the project and incubating this pilot program, let's call it on a sort of part-time basis, I'd been talking to my boss [Howard Averill], who at that time was the CFO of the Television Group . . . we were talking about what I was doing and I was talking about the education project and he asked me another series of questions—"What's the business model? And what's the revenue potential? And what're the investments?" I didn't have answers to any of those questions and he said, "You know what? Stop. You're wasting your time. Just don't do this. Just forget it. This is a distraction, you've got more important things to worry about, so don't do it." And I left the room and I thought, "With all due respect (because he's a very bright individual), he doesn't get it. He doesn't realize how important this is, so I'm going to keep doing it."

After about three or four months, it again had come up in conversation and he said, "Are we talking about that education thing?" And I said, "We are." And he said, "Why are we talking about that? That was killed months ago." And I said, "That actually wasn't." And he said, "Well, that's a problem." So I said, "Let's now have a rational conversation about it and I'll show you what we've been doing." When he saw it he said, "OK. I get the value equation. I see the value, but you be very, very careful here. Don't lose a ton of money."

Jones was up against a headcount freeze when he hired those sixty producers, but he managed some financial wizardry in order to spread his budget around on less-experienced producers who nonetheless were more familiar with new media. He continued to incubate the project, keeping an eye on the bottom line, until Averill left the NBC Television group for Time Warner. Once again, Jones found himself defending the project—this time to his new boss, NBC-Universal CFO Lynn Calpeter:

Again, it became fairly quickly obvious that this project was losing money, so I was called up to her office on the executive floors to explain what was going on—it was clear by that time we had probably invested a few million dollars, and that [it] would automatically be shut down. So I went. I walked into the boardroom and again, she had largely some of the same questions that Howard had had, and I still didn't have all the answers. She said, "Well, how much money is this going to cost? Show me the forecast for the next twelve to eighteen months." And I said, "I want you to see the demo first." She said, "No, I haven't got time. How much is this going to lose?" I said, "I want to show the demo first." She said, "I'm too busy, how much is this going to lose?" And I thought, "If I tell her, she's going to kill it." So I said, "I'm not going to show the numbers until you've seen it." So she saw the demo, and she was absolutely blown away. She said, "This is extraordinary stuff. I have to say, before you walked in here, I was going to shut it down, but now I've seen it. I see the potential. So, in a very managed way—and you better not lose a lot of money on this—proceed with caution." I feel that we skirted danger so much with this project from the outset.

This conversation, in many ways, exemplifies the battle that iCue faced along the way. There were demands for projects twelve to eighteen months away, a time period that may be normal or even long in the broadcast media business. But in the land of education innovation, where even revolutions (as opposed to evolutions) can take a decade to take hold, twelve to eighteen months is extremely aggressive. To Jones, though, at this point, the idea was the thing. The innovation was what could convince the executives to get behind the project, or at least not block his way. They knew innovation when they saw it, but they didn't know the challenges of the education market. All along, it had been clear that iCue was going to be a difficult proposition to pursue, and Jones was sure that his team wasn't going to be able to go it alone.

6 Television Dollars and Digital Pennies

In truth, the biggest hurdle is still the business model. Although every executive who has seen the proposal and watched it evolve in recent months insists that we have to do it, the $14 million pill to make it happen is more than anyone wants to swallow. Somebody get me a glass of water! So, I've been working to adjust the business model and think I've struck upon a combination of school- and student-subscription levels that are complemented by some generous sponsorship support. I've sent those numbers to the business development folks as of last night and will be working on profit-loss projections when I return to New York tomorrow. I'm very encouraged by the new matrix and think the executives will find it a much easier marketing proposition, especially when we go to market in partnership with the *New York Times* and the College Board.

—Alex Chisholm

Sadly, iCue's financial problems would not be solved when Alex wrote the above—October 2006. The mounting cost of producing the material iCue needed in order to be competitive and fully realized meant that iCue would undergo some dramatic shifts. There was a clear need to sustain the product with immediate cash infusions while work to turn the archives into a viable educational product continued. From NBC's perspective, the clear goal of iCue was to capture a new, online audience and to do it by making inroads into education with NBC's ample archives. In order to do this, NBC knew it meant not only changing the content and format, but changing where and how NBC News got in front of young viewers (or viewers, period). As it tried to move from a top-down broadcast way of thinking to a more participatory model and to find a sustainable business model in a (for NBC) untested market, iCue's final product would come to be heavily influenced by these challenges and the search for solutions.

The Advanced Placement Market

The early designs that Chisholm and Carol Williams pitched in 2006 for what became iCue were based on meeting young people where they already were and where the trends seemed to be heading— video, games, and social networking. Although these media were relevant to most high schoolers (and a growing segment of middle schoolers), the initial target market was AP students, their parents, and their teachers. The national curriculum and the tendency to invest in supplementary educational materials meant that this market might be inclined to buy this particular product, as opposed to many other educational markets that were accustomed to receiving everything for free from ad-supported sites, foundations, or textbook company giveaways such as online workbooks. As a result, Jones and Chisholm began discussions with the College Board (the purveyors of the AP exam) early in the life of iCue. Early on, things looked promising, as the College Board seemed excited about the project.

Meanwhile, the project was being designed and populated with content as quickly as the rapidly growing team could manage. As negotiations with partners including the College Board were taking place, the question of how iCue would reach the AP audience, and exactly how this would be monetized, loomed large. The original goal for the project was to market directly to consumers, as any other test-preparation product or homework aid would be. The product would have to promise to raise scores or grades and be worth the money that students (or more likely their parents) would spend on it. Students in the Digital Design Squads seemed most inclined to use the site as a means for raising their test scores, rather than as place to hang out and discuss school topics out of love for the topics. Regarding an early focus test with a group of AP and honors students, Chisholm wrote:

Reaction to the overall concept was generally positive. We have some issues to address in terms of marketing and pricing, but I think we can handle those (having done dozens of focus groups, pricing never comes out where you think it will or want it).

The other big thing we need to be mindful of is that although the site will be kid-directed, it really does need to be teacher-parent-approved, which we can manage in our marketing efforts. I'm not worried about that, although it goes somewhat counter to some of our experiences in this area. They also recommended multiple "authentic" print news sources be part of the experience because their teachers will like that. As an "information resource" alone, they kids saw tremendous value in supporting their schoolwork.

Early on in the process, then, students were already thinking of the project as something their teachers would need to approve of or be invested in. Having multiple content partners in print and video could be a means of meeting the curricular needs of history teachers, who regularly connect students with the past by providing a number of primary sources and compelling the students to interpret the discrepancies and similarities among the sources. It would also make them attractive to the College Board, whose exams typically include document-based questions (DBQs), described by the College Board thus: "The required DBQ differs from the standard essays in its emphasis on your ability to analyze and synthesize historical data and assess verbal, quantitative, or pictorial materials as historical evidence. Like the standard essays, however, the DBQ is judged on its thesis and argument" (APCentral, n.d.). But perhaps even more important for Jones, partnering with other media companies could distribute the cost and reduce the risk seen by each of the partners. Chisholm had been looking for print partners even before the project was committed to NBC News:

In June of 2006, I met a woman, Cathy Mahoney, [from] the *New York Times* at a conference in Shanghai, and she had been delivering a research paper . . . on how the *New York Times* had begun to track articles that were being blogged and/or emailed, and what that meant in terms of how they thought about placement of articles and the syndication and subscription and their business model for moving content.

And so after I heard that paper, two weeks later she and I had a luncheon meeting in New York, and I pitched [the iCue project] to her. . . . So I wasn't just thinking about a network, even though I was thinking about video archives, thinking about the *New York Times* as another partner in this was really a great opportunity. So that was what really pushed things into high gear in June of 2006, was that I had his other major media company that was looking at it—that was looking at what they could do with their archives in education, and I thought that I'd be this fantastic matchmaker between [print and video media].

The desire to blend and mix various media with technology was of course a logical outgrowth of Chisholm's Comparative Media Studies background. Chisholm and Williams started to pursue the *Washington Post* as well. Williams was inspired to seek out its archives because of the power of the Watergate material, but the team realized that because the

Washington Post had owned *Newsweek* since 1961, it could also be on the road to acquiring more long-form, magazine-style content, which would at least benefit the English language and composition section.

The negotiations with these print partners dragged on for months, however, so the team had to continue to pursue other possibilities for funding and, as a result, what type of offering iCue would be. The major alternative was that the product could be sold to teachers and schools. A school would purchase the product and then provide access to the students in the school. This model meant fewer and larger sales, and it raised the question of just how you sell to those markets. And every business model for either market was going to result in at least some amount of reconfiguring of the site's feature list and functionality.

The early decision about which model to pursue was ultimately not to decide, even as the team spent a tremendous amount of money transforming the archives. Instead, the team developed a product that could theoretically either be sold direct to students as supplementary materials or be sold to schools and teachers as a classroom-based product. With that latter audience in mind, some teacher focus groups were formed to get feedback on the early designs. As excited as they were about the idea of iCue and some of the content, they seemed to raise as many questions about implementation as they answered about engaging students with the content. "We really took a step back after that meeting to think about what are the things that should be in the scope," stated then technical lead Michael Levin, "like personal messag[ing] was out for iCue, as one example. Photos, like personal photos [were out], and we ended up going with avatars . . . and fake names versus real names. We ended up having a lot more security and taking out features and things to comply with some of the concerns that we heard from teachers." Although some of those originally intended features might have been fine for the direct-to-consumer model for teenagers, they were not acceptable for teachers. Those features never made it to the implementation phase in order to keep both markets (again, theoretically) viable.

As the production teams tried to walk the line between a consumer product and an institutional one, conversations continued with the College Board. Meetings with the College Board consistently went well—the board loved the product and thought it served a unique purpose. But, as Jones describes, the College Board thought it was so useful that NBC News should "just give it all away." This strategy was appealing to Jones in some ways, but was a nonstarter as the basis of a for-profit venture—there was no clear path to sustainability. Despite these disagreements with the College Board, the team was already committed to the AP pathway for iCue. It had matched archival content to and created new content for the AP curricula, and it had developed features for the site that closely matched the features of the AP exams. Negotiations came to an unsuccessful close with the College Board, and due to the tight connection to the AP exams, NBC News had to license question banks from the AP exams to use in iCue. Similarly, NBC would not be able to convince the *New York Times* or the *Washington Post* to share the cost of producing iCue, so it ended up also licensing content from those newspapers to flesh out the iCue archive, adding even more to iCue's growing costs. Through the middle of 2007, Chisholm and Jones would try to prop up the direct-to-consumer model with other funding partners, through foundations such as Intel and Hewlett as well as private equity firms, but nothing ever came together. Even though all of these agencies reported excitement about the ideas, no one wanted to take the risk. A student-centric marketing model was all but doomed, and a teacher-centric, institutional model started moving front and center.

A Different Type of Partner

The College Board wasn't being looked at as supplemental, but more as kind of the traction, and that additional content that could be used to set up what the framework of the experience was. . . . There were stipulations that Adam started talking about in July, in terms of, "We need the College Board and/or a publisher, and so obviously, a textbook publisher." We had this sense that, in addition to the raw materials of the video and *New York Times* articles and *Washington Post* articles, that you could literally cut up textbooks [for CueCards] and have those operate in the system the same way, so that you could see textbook snippets, but the condensed versions were the ones that had been editorialized and had made sense of all the source material, you could look at those snippets and further tie it to what was happening in the classroom.

—Alex Chisholm

As the direct-to-consumer model began to wane in the eyes of the leadership, the focus shifted heavily once again to bringing on a textbook publisher as a partner. This move would not only bring more content, but add another important piece that was key to the project's evolving direction:

an established distribution partner with the "traction" with schools that was lost when negotiations with the College Board fell through. The vast majority of educational purchasing in schools happens through textbook publishers, so if the iCue team wanted to get into schools, that was the way in. As Chisholm reports, though, textbook publishers would prove to be yet more potential partners who, though curious and excited about the idea of iCue, could not make the right commitment:

The distribution is the no-brainer. You needed a pipeline into the schools. The challenge was that the textbook companies have this legacy business—the investment in a [physical, paper-based] textbook, and then all of the technology [is] built onto it. . . .

So Jeff Zucker and Dick Ebersol, especially in relation to the Olympics, are always talking about *television dollars* and *digital pennies*. The same holds true in the textbook market—they invest all this money in these basal textbooks, and yet the technology that they've built has all these requirements about single sign-on and assessment and all of the pieces that teachers and districts require for the way that money— that state money or local money—is allocated . . . unless it fits within their single sign-on domain or environment, they couldn't do it. They also . . . had a real problem with all this other media and the social networking aspect of it. There were so many things that just didn't work within the traditional textbook publishing business structure that it just became insurmountable.

For all these reasons, the textbook publishers never came on board. The team's efforts to build a coalition of partners to support and distribute iCue had failed. Despite their combined expertise in business and in educational technology, a business development plan simply was not cohering. Suspecting that they might need a new type of expertise on the team, Jones made a new hire in March 2007.

Bring in the Marketing

They really believed that because they were going into education, and they weren't an education company, they really needed an education partner. So that's when Adam got it in his head that he needed to find a textbook marketer. . . . Nicola [Soares] was part of a team at McGraw-Hill that we met in or October of 2006. We were making the rounds to Pearson and McGraw-Hill; those were the two big [textbook publishers] that we were meeting with. And I remember Nicola at a meeting, and she seemed discontented with her colleagues. She seemed to be saying the right things . . . then by March Adam told me he had hired her.

—Alex Chisholm

Nicola Soares, a vice president of product innovation at McGraw-Hill, was among the textbook personnel who had seen iCue as it made the rounds searching for development and distribution partners. Without these partner organizations and with the attendant shift in iCue's designated market, Jones was in need of someone to head up these new marketing efforts. Specifically, he needed someone with expertise in marketing to schools. Although the textbook world was not known for its innovation, it certainly was known for being able to market to schools. Soares fit the bill, having grown weary of the lack of innovation in textbooks, and saw great opportunity in the project that Jones was championing.

Soares had begun her career as a social studies teacher at the middle and high school levels in Virginia, in the innovative district of Lynchburg. From her start in the early 1990s, that district was relying more on digital resources than on textbooks, and she had an opportunity to be an early pioneer in teaching with digital resources. After a move to Columbus, Ohio, in 1996, Soares moved from the classroom to McGraw-Hill, where she headed up a project creating a book on using Internet resources in social studies classes. She stayed on at McGraw-Hill for over a decade, working in editorial project management in instructional technology, language arts, and social sciences, eventually being promoted to vice president for product innovation, overseeing much of the company's digital media across disciplines. In that role, in which she oversaw partnerships, she met Jones and was drawn to iCue, attracted to its innovative ideas like the rest of the iCue team's leaders.

Soares officially joined iCue in May 2007, when "millions of dollars had already been spent." Jones believed that the fresh perspective from someone who knew how to sell digital products to schools could solve his "distribution problem." Soares quickly realized that iCue was having market identity problems, not knowing which market to serve—the consumer or the school. As a result, it wasn't serving either of them well. She says:

When I entered, there was not really a plan or know-how to directly market iCue. At that point, they wanted it to be sort of a free consumer [model]. Maybe [it would] generate revenue with online advertising. But [it was] also an institutional model that would be sold by subscription into the school market. And primarily the target audience of iCue . . . was Advanced Placement students. So, looking from a business perspective of what had been spent and what the company would expect [as a] return on investment, it would never pay the bills. . . . The percentage of kids that actually participate and are enrolled in AP courses is less than 1 percent here in this country.

So the first problem from Soares's perspective was that there were dueling identities. And the second was that the AP market was too small to be successful. iCue could never generate the revenue it required by catering solely to the AP market, especially in light of the skyrocketing digitization and production costs:

I also felt that it was sort of limited in its target audience. And why wouldn't something that great be opened up to the mainstream? All students, of all ability levels? Because when you actually looked at the archival content, and given what a news organization does every day, reporting and teaching "the first draft of history," if you will, it would be beneficial to all students and certainly the head learners of the classroom, teachers.

Almost immediately, the team was faced with the question of how to expand beyond the AP market. Shining the spotlight more squarely on schools and teachers raised many questions of how this decentralized, student-focused product was supposed to mesh with the practices and policies of schools and classrooms. As social networks were dawning, so too were questions of how young people should participate in those networks. Teacher focus groups were quick to raise many questions about this participation. Levin recalled some of those focus groups that Soares brought in:

I can recall a lot of the concerns by teachers during the focus groups around the moderation aspects of iCue. They were really concerned that that would be adding to their job or their responsibilities for monitoring what the students were doing in the community—what they were talking about in discussion forums, what they were messaging to one another, notes and things they would be putting on CueCards. . . . It seemed like it was going to be a burden to them, an additional burden. And that's sort of what influenced our decision on taking out of some of the features of what we had originally planned to do.

But Levin also commented on other pressures that were emerging at that time:

Nicola [Soares], at the time [she was hired], really wanted us to get something . . . to market now—like in four weeks, six weeks. She said, "We need to have something for the launch of the school year, and I'm going to hire a sales team. I can't wait for iCue to be what it needs to be from a student perspective so we need something now."

The synchronization of the development cycle and sales cycle with schools' academic year–based adoption cycle was a real concern that needed to be factored in. Missing that cycle might put the project another year behind in its opportunity to get paying institutional customers.

With these new stressors at hand, iCue reached its first fork in the road and split in two. Although part of the efforts continued to focus on the iCue product for the AP market, another effort was launched to reach more teachers in more subjects more quickly, with fewer of the complexities that iCue introduced. This change meant fewer of the originally designed, more innovative features. The new product, a fork of iCue, to be developed by the same team, became known as "Archives on Demand." Principally, it was a Spartan bank of tagged video clips in the form of CueCards that could be used in classrooms.

As a result of the push to get something to market quickly for cash-flow reasons, it was inevitable that Archives on Demand would become not just a moneymaking splinter, but a full-fledged product on its own. Levin commented:

Nicola Soares' idea was that iCue was too far ahead of its time, that it was too "consumerish," that schools wouldn't adopt it. It didn't meet some of the institutional requirements that schools would need. It was too student-centric. . . . So the products began to segment themselves. We ended up segmenting our business. As the business strategy evolved, the product strategy evolved as well. And so we ended up having not just iCue, but we had Archives on Demand, which was sort of competing, in a way, with iCue.

Archives on Demand was really just a limited form of iCue, repurposing not only the video footage, but the metadata, the licenses that Jones had procured, and much of the underlying technology as well. Levin notes, "And that's when we built the full-page video player for Archives on Demand. We built that in four weeks because we were repurposing existing technology that was here at NBC, it was something that could be spun up fairly quickly, and so we used that initially."

But redesigning the product was only part of the solution. NBC News still needed a quick win with the product—something that would get out quickly to a large audience and bring in some revenue to keep the iCue ship afloat. As Jones and Soares searched for potential partners, they entered discussions with HotChalk, an ad-supported website hosting a learning-management system targeted at K–12 teachers. At the time, HotChalk served about 25,000 teachers around the country as an easy-to-use tool for managing their classes. Having only just opened for business early in 2007, it was one of the most rapidly growing education websites at the time. Teachers could organize their syllabi, link to resources, and distribute materials to students. HotChalk's own materials at the time described the resource thus: "The HotChalk Learning Environment includes curriculum management, lesson plan development, and secure email, as well as automated assignment distribution, collection, and grading in a web-based environment" (HotChalk 2010). HotChalk was not only a classroom space; it was also a social network over which teachers shared curricula and obtained access to classroom materials, similar to the listservs Beth Nissen had visited to help create the AP English curriculum for iCue. And that was where NBC News fit in. It could distribute its digital archives through HotChalk for a fee, for teachers to use in their classes or in their online syllabi.

Jones started to hammer out a deal with HotChalk in which HotChalk would become the exclusive means by which limited Archives on Demand content could be distributed initially for free to teachers. Over time, this free-subscription model would expire and be replaced by a paid subscription, through an institutionwide site license. Access to the resource would, it was hoped, drive more people to the ad-supported HotChalk, bringing it revenue as well. The goal was that HotChalk would not only provide short-term revenue through the deal, but also be a stand-in for the sales force that NBC News didn't have. Jones recalled the early deal with HotChalk: "I liked HotChalk because their model had been creating lesson plans by teachers that were then shared, so it's almost like a social network of teachers basically, sharing, creating resources and sharing them. So I thought that's a great way to marry the content."

But a couple of problems needed to be solved immediately in order to make the deal work. Most of these, Jones recounted, focused on the traditional, teacher-centered needs of HotChalk's audience:

The first [problem] was that we had to have state standard correlation because obviously that would make it relevant. . . . [B]eing able to leverage the metadata that we created, we found that the metadata correlation to state standards was actually fairly straightforward. Expensive, but we just did it because the metadata [were] so strong. So again, you make the right investment up front. The second [problem] was that there were significant barriers to the use of streaming video in the classroom based on infrastructure and bandwidth. Therefore, we would have to have a download solution. Now obviously I had already anticipated clearing the resources for download, but it was just an additional complication in terms of delivering the product.

Levin looked back on these requirements that ultimately worked their way into the product, and regretted not getting them in there from the start:

Institutional features like state standards features, like download features, ended up as things that would end up going into Archives on Demand. But to be honest, if I went back the original business requirements for iCue, I can tell you state standards [were] definitely not in there. . . . And looking back on it, [they] should have been there. [They] really should have been there as a way to really be a forcing function. What I've found with state standards up to this point is that—it's the same effect that you get of when someone sees the CueCard for the first time, where their jaws drop. You get a similar reaction when people see state standards.

Soares agreed; the standards were a necessary component. Although the team may have wished teachers to have the freedom and flexibility to construct the curriculum as they pleased, the reality was that without the connection to standards, teachers wouldn't adopt it:

Having to correlate content to state standards . . . we have this really irritating thing of "high stakes in all fifty states." And I said, "I know it's awful, but we have to do it." It's a "check-off" kind of a thing, because our kids are tested. It's unfortunate but [leaving state standards as a] "nice to have" is not going to get us in a position where we can actually get our students and teachers using this stuff. You have to have some of those things that teachers are mandated to use.

Additionally, Jones realized that the core set of three AP courses would be insufficient for supporting the video content in a broader K–12 market. That meant creating more courses and more content at a significant cost.

As the HotChalk deal was hashed out, iCue continued to roll on in parallel, causing some confusion on both the development and marketing sides as to what they were doing and for whom. That confusion about direction was symptomatic of greater troubles. Around that time, much of the project started to unravel. The startup team of Williams and Chisholm was out for different reasons, which meant a loss of vision as well as of morale. The Archives on Demand project, through HotChalk, held promise as a revenue stream, but in the short term it would require a significant investment in order to create content that was broad enough and also align with standards in all fifty states. Thus the best-case scenarios for profitability were further off.

7 Ever More Desperate Attempts

The forks in the road and the creation of a new product would set the tone for the middle phase of iCue's development. In 2007 and early 2008, that development was dominated by the utter confusion over what iCue could or should be. The Archives on Demand project and the partnership with HotChalk were ostensibly going to create a revenue stream to sustain the development of the more innovative iCue product. iCue was going to bring young people to NBC News as viewers and participants. But it became clear that iCue had to serve teachers better, and it had to serve more than Advanced Placement students, despite the work that had been put into aligning the archives with the AP curriculum. NBC News was going to find itself looking hard at whom it was trying to serve, how it was trying to serve them, and what the boundaries of its projects were.

HotChalk? WTF?

As NBC News went forward with the HotChalk deal (including a later financial stake in HotChalk to foster its growth), the Education Arcade was growing anxious about the new direction of the project and the fate of iCue. Unable to support the project design on a day-to-day basis from Massachusetts, TEA was unable to contribute meaningfully or in a timely way to these ongoing debates. Chisholm, now working primarily from the sidelines, was focused on traveling around with other NBC News staff members, trying to find more money to create a viable subscription model for iCue, when he heard the news:

And we were having conversations with private equity groups to try to fund this thing and back-stop it, and I get the notice that Nicola [Soares] is being hired, and then I get this notice that we're having a meeting with this company called HotChalk, which is when I came to. I was like, "What the fuck is HotChalk?!" . . .

[J]ust as that check and that agreement was being put together, Adam sent me an email and asked me what he should do about HotChalk, whether he should walk away or not. And I said, "I don't know that you should walk away; I just think you should be really cautious, because I don't know what this guy's motivations are. I don't know what's in it for us yet, because they don't have this market space . . . my colleagues have never heard of them, the teachers that I work with have never heard of them. I don't know what this is."

Chisholm was understandably upset that his brainchild was suddenly being hitched to a small, relatively unknown player in the educational technology space with a traditional teacher-focused delivery model. Moreover, the creation of the Archives on Demand product threatened the existence of iCue. No one was indicating as much, and indeed, at the beginning of the summer of 2007, preparations were being made for the soft launch and to debut the product at the AP teachers' conference in Las Vegas. That summer, the *New York Times* (by then a licensed content partner) did a story on iCue as a promotion for the soft launch. The article was strongly focused on reaching a new audience with archival material, but there was no mention of the site's games, and the social-networking aspect of the site was buried in the second-to-last paragraph.

It was starting to become clear that NBC's internal narrative heavily favored a product to be sold to schools, and that was almost certainly a death knell for features such as social networking that were, at the time, highly controversial. In an effort to create a case for iCue's more innovative aspects—the games and social networking, as well as even more exciting endeavors such as mentored media production—the Education Arcade proposed a twofold strategy. First, it would conduct a model journalism competition in which students would, through the library in Reading, Massachusetts, tell stories about their local communities with support and mentoring from NBC News professionals. Second, it would develop a white paper about using these tools in the classroom in order to connect teachers with best practices for using social-networking technology and games at school. The goal of the first project was to demonstrate the value of connecting with passionate teen media producers for NBC News, and the value of the second piece would be to demonstrate to teachers the wisdom of adopting innovative technologies in spite of the real and imagined risks involved. It was unclear whether these projects would be enough to sustain the long-term viability of a fully interactive iCue, steeped in the tenets of participatory culture and new media literacy, but they seemed to be the only options. The white paper would help build an audience in schools and the journalism competition would allow NBC News to experience the value of directly connecting with its presumed target audience of online teens. It wouldn't become clear until later just how out of the loop TEA was and how naïve this approach would be.

MIT-NBC News Reading Journalism Competition

The journalism competition was implemented in a racially and economically diverse town within driving distance of MIT whose library was working hard to become a technologically savvy community center. The library was already making strong headway in attracting a teen demographic by holding events such as manga illustration and video game nights.

The competition (see advertisement in figure 7.1) attracted twelve participants, some working together but most working alone, most of whom turned in completed work. The stipulations for the competition pieces were these:

• Tell a local news story that is meaningful to you, and try to connect it to a national story.

• You can tell that story however you want—video, podcast, photo essay, text—so long as that medium can be uploaded to the Internet.

• Pieces should be no longer than five minutes.

Over the course of four weeks, competitors were supported in their project work by iCue team members with backgrounds in journalism via a Facebook group (before Facebook stopped supporting this functionality), as well as in three seminar-style meetings with iCue design wizard and former documentary producer Kathy Abbott. Abbott appeared once in person and twice via video conferencing software. MIT researchers also camped out at the library twice a week in order to provide technical support for various media technologies and to answer competition questions. The winning team produced an extremely professional piece of video journalism (figures 7.2 and 7.3) about a family that moved into a Habitat for Humanity home in Reading. As their prize, the team members

GOT A STORY TO TELL?

This summer, high schoolers over 13 who live in ▮▮▮ or go to school here can participate in a journalism competition presented in association with MIT and NBC NEWS!

Kick Off / Sign Up Meeting 6:00 P.M. on July,16, 2007
in the ▮▮▮ Public Library Meeting Room

For more information, contact the ▮▮▮ Public
Library InformationDesk, ▮▮▮

NBC NEWS   MIT Massachusetts Institute of Technology   . Coordinating Librarians: ▮▮▮ and ▮▮▮

Figure 7.1
Recruitment poster for the journalism competition kickoff targeting teens.

Figure 7.2
A member of the winning team as "on-air" talent in front of the Habitat for Humanity house in the story.

Figure 7.3
The production values of the winning team's entry, as evidenced by a pull-back from a map to outer space. (Those are clouds in the foreground.)

visited the set of *Nightly News* that fall (after their college applications were turned in).

The competition successfully provided NBC News with a rough draft of how it might proceed in media mentorship, and how it might produce real value for its target audience. The Facebook group was definitely used, mostly by the members of the winning team, as evidenced by the following post:

A midnight question—(Woohoo for sleep deprivation!)

In the instance of Habitat—do we go looking for opposition to the project (for example asking questions like "Did you recieve [sic] any complaints or negative feed back [sic]" or "Did you have any negative opinion of the project on the whole?")

Or do we ask more generally "how did people respond to this project?" or "how do you feel about this project?"—and let the people answer for themselves in which case if we don't receive any negativity we don't go looking for it.

I'm personally inclined to go with the latter, but I was just wondering what your thoughts were—Thanks!

Real learning was happening, and a mentoring relationship definitely evolved over the course of the competition. It would be easy to imagine that even stronger relationships could evolve over time within a "studio" space for media creation within iCue. Abbott and the iCue staff members who participated enjoyed meeting with the students. Ultimately, though, the competition did not meet the Education Arcade's goals—the competition created extra work for an already taxed iCue team and did not provide sufficient value to change the course of production. While meeting with students and coordinating the judging of the competition, Abbott was also working hard on the site's look and feel and preparing for the soft launch at the Advanced Placement conference in Las Vegas. The staff members who participated were under tremendous pressure to continue producing assets in order to meet Soares's September deadline. In follow-up responses, it would be clear that NBC News was pleased to be able to have done the work supporting the competition, and was perhaps even interested in being able to do more, but not any time soon.

Educating Educators

The white paper, *Using the Technology of Today in the Classroom of Today* (Klopfer et al. 2009), was made available to NBC News several times over the course of its development, but the full paper was not officially released until February 12, 2009—too late to be a tool for audience building for iCue. An abridged version of the paper was released in the fall of 2008 in the journal *Learning and Leading with Technology* (Groff and Haas 2008). The paper has nevertheless proved a popular resource since its debut. It has already been downloaded nearly a million times, was the second resource Google pointed to for "classroom technology," and was ranked as one of the top one hundred learning games resources by the Upside Learning blog in early 2011.

The paper has three major components. It begins by addressing the existing research in technologies with potential for the classroom, building heavily on the work of James Paul Gee and the New Media Literacies group and relating those ideas and theories to practical uses for and the affordances of specific games and tools, ranging from the massively multiplayer online role-playing game World of Warcraft to the personal social network–creating tool Ning. The paper then focuses, in two parts, on ways to adopt new technologies. The first portion presents and builds on the i5 (Individualized Inventory for Integrating Instructional Innovations)—a tool developed by one of the paper's coauthors, Jennifer Groff, and her graduate school advisor, Chrystalla Mouza (see Groff and Mouza 2008). This framework helps teachers more successfully integrate learning technologies into

their classrooms by aiding them in identifying likely barriers they will
encounter when teaching with the new learning tool. The tool focuses on
four major areas where teachers can typically be stymied by innovations
and helps them improve their likelihood of success in those areas: in their
Contexts (the schools or districts in which they teach), as *Innovators* (identifying their own abilities and comfort zones), with the *Operators* (their
students), and with the *Innovation* (the technology itself). Before adopting
a new learning technology for the classroom, a teacher can go through the
various elements of the i5 and take stock of his or her position, potential
challenges, and strengths in each of the four areas. By being aware of and
addressing likely barriers and challenges ahead of time, the teacher can
then take steps to mitigate them in order to have more success with the
innovation. The tool includes recommendations about common challenges a teacher may face. For instance, if the teacher's own abilities are a
limiting factor, the teacher could seek out help from a tech-savvy colleague
or the school's IT director.

The second, implementation-focused part of the white paper connects
the tools and ideas to best practices already adopted by innovative teachers
using technology in their classrooms. By highlighting the practices of a
social studies teacher who uses the notoriously involved board game Diplo-
macy to teach history, or a pair of teachers who support each other in the
use of software to create ecological simulations in the classroom, the paper
makes a case for the use of these tools. Another teacher cited in the piece
makes the argument that using these tools in the classroom not only aids
his instruction, but allows him to help his students navigate these new
technological waters, which is important to him.

A Moment in History

Meanwhile, back at NBC, the two distinct products were barreling ahead—
iCue and the Archives on Demand. Producer Soraya Gage notes, "We were
building two different websites too. We were building the iCue website,
and then we were building a more mass-market website. iCue was too
'niche' to be really profitable for us. . . . So simultaneously, we were adding
metadata to two different content-management systems."

While future revenue streams were looking more likely to be associated
with the branch that had become Archives on Demand than with iCue,

there was still an internal effort afoot to promote iCue and make it a flag-ship product. In early 2008, Jones—eager to keep the iCue property alive—thought the team might be able to create another reason for visitors to come to the iCue site. He says:

2008 is probably a fairly unique moment in time because this election is going to be historic for a number of reasons, not only could [there] be the first African American president in the White House, but we have an opportunity to really engage an audience. . . . So we decided we would supplement the three courses in iCue, the ones we built as templates, with a fourth one called Decision '08. Decision '08 would be our major driver in 2008. . . . [Now] there's a weekly reason to come back to iCue through Decision '08, albeit not obviously correlated to curriculum. But if you've got people coming into iCue to look at Decision '08 and they see this core content wrapped around history. . . . So we [launched] iCue at the end of April 2008 with the four courses in it.

Soares from marketing also liked the idea of an election-focused module within iCue, "I said, 'All right, launch with Decision '08,' thinking back on what MSNBC was doing. That will get us ready for Government and Politics as the first course to go out." But she also realized that the market that Decision '08 might attract could be significantly different from the one for the rest of the courses:

I said, "But understand you're going to get—because this is a consumer product—you're going to get an older audience that might consume it and be very interested in it as well." I said, "I actually think it's a really phenomenal thing if we have all people of all different ages actually using it. . . . The more people who were online or using social media or involved in the gaming . . . why not?"

So the Decision '08 module was around at the full launch of iCue in the spring of 2008. As expected, it brought a substantially different audience. A more complete analysis of the site-usage data is found in chapter 10.

Facebook

Even before the data were in, it was apparent to the NBC News team that iCue wasn't attracting a large enough audience to its site, nor was it attract-ing the audience of young viewers that it had hoped to. In 2008, as the Digital Design Squads had already pointed out, where better to look for a young audience than on the increasingly popular Facebook? Having learned some lessons about what it didn't know about social media and games, this time the team looked outside the organization for help. Technical lead Michael Levin describes the search:

So that's when we went external to a social media group in downtown called Appssavvy, who specialize in selling social media. They were selling games like the Biggest Brain in Facebook. . . . They built their start-up—their entire sales team and sales model—around selling social media. We showed them iCue. [We] first brought them in here, showed them iCue, and showed them our idea for *What's Your iCue* in Facebook, and they said, "This is phenomenal, this is great—we think that we can help sell this for you guys before it's even built."

But, like everything else, the Facebook game was not free to develop. Although the designers were able to repurpose much of the work that they had done, the project did take some additional development. Further, the Facebook game, and the visibility that it could offer, became an opportunity to bring in some much-needed revenue through additional partnerships. This aspect was important, because the HotChalk deal had started to go down in flames. Although the free subscriptions to the NBC News content helped fuel the rapid growth of HotChalk by nearly 500 percent over the course of the first year, the conversion to paid customers never happened. At $1,500 to $2,000 per school, the market that HotChalk was supposed to drive to paid content never materialized. This lack might have been because the price was too high, because there weren't enough subscribed or interested teachers in any one school to justify the expense, because the company couldn't reach the people with purchasing power, or because of any number of other logistical reasons. HotChalk had not been the de facto sales force that Jones had hoped for, particularly after HotChalk essentially dismantled its own sales force. Now, instead of the solid, sustaining revenue stream NBC News had wanted, it had generated a new product with yet another significant associated cost.

Fortunately, the team at Appssavvy was correct, and it was indeed able to sell the Facebook game to sponsors—Lexus and the University of Phoenix, initially. Although the connection to Lexus might merely have been the target demographic of online video-based Facebook trivia games (likely an educated older audience), the connection with the University of Phoenix was more significant. Jones points to the key role that the University of Phoenix played not only in launching the Facebook game, but in shoring up the iCue team's efforts generally:

I pared back the body of content on iCue so that I could have clear differentiation. Because of the economics, I would have to focus on my subscription resource—I was unable to keep investing in and building out iCue. . . . We continued to do some experimentation around iCue . . . because we weren't getting enough penetration at the teen and preteen level, [and I decided] I would go and find them. Obviously, the way to find them is to go to Facebook.

So we launched a Facebook game called *What's Your iCue?* . . . which in itself was kind of a cool thing to do, but I managed to get it sponsored by the University of Phoenix. Then, having met the University of Phoenix, [we] had the chance to talk about iCue and they liked the concept . . . they totally got iCue like no one else has.

Continued Diversification

The product that was originally iCue continued to diversify. iCue itself remained a space that combined games and social networking (albeit scaled back from the original designs, as Jones indicates) with the content from the NBC News archives. iCue still targeted the original set of AP courses and Decision '08, although by mid-2010, it had added an environmental science course and a special collection on civil rights. But the strategy of NBC News—to engage an audience through online learning and video—had clearly extended well beyond that. From the largely adult audience of Decision '08 to the general school-based K–12 market that the Archives on Demand attracted to the postsecondary-school market that the Facebook game started to draw in, NBC News had cast an ever wider net for potential markets and sources of revenue. It would continue to nurture those markets and scout new markets as well. Jones discussed the need to cast that much-broader net:

The economic necessity suggested that we should be as broad-based as possible and we should look at a K-20 spectrum. . . . And that's obvious. There's just a general tsunami of change as multimedia instruction becomes a more important component of education. That's going to happen. But we can play our part to drive that.

And just like that, NBC News was now looking to extend its reach to colleges. No matter how wide a net Jones cast, though, he maintained an eye on the dream that motivated this journey—facilitating youth participation with his brand. All of the scrambling and revenue-chasing performed during 2007 and 2008 were in the service of feeding iCue, the participatory product. From his perspective, the Education Arcade's white paper and journalism competition didn't fall on deaf ears; they just couldn't change the bottom line.

Education became the single market, the way forward for NBC News in the eyes of Jones and his team. But it wasn't *just* a market they were serving, nor was it *just* a resource they were building; education had become a calling. Jones was talking like a believer.

8 The Hype

From: Capus, Steve (NBC Universal)
Sent: Friday, August 10, 2007, 10:30 am
To: @NBC Uni News Everyone; @MSNBC Everyone (NBC Uni MSNBC)
Cc: Zucker, Jeff (NBC Universal)
Subject: iCue

In advance of its official launch next week, I am very pleased to introduce iCue, a major digital initiative for NBC News that will raise the bar for educational digital content used in schools across America. At the same time iCue will help transform NBC News. . . .

In addition to giving you a preview of iCue, I want to share with you that the NBC News video archives will be going live online in the HotChalk Learning Community at the fingertips of educators in more than 20% of US K-12 Schools. Through our partnership with HotChalk, NBC News' rich video content captured and created over 60+ years is being delivered to more than 100,000 schools across the country. In the months to come, we plan to build upon this dynamic partnership further when both iCue and NBC News' video archives are available through the HotChalk Learning Community.

The richness of the NBC News archives combined with the unique features of iCue creates a very sophisticated, engaging and elegant learning resource that we can all be proud of. This is yet another example of a digital initiative in which NBC News is reinventing itself and developing its content to reach a brand new audience.

We pre-launched iCue last month in Las Vegas at the Advanced Placement Annual Conference hosted by the College Board and the response was overwhelming. Teachers of US History, US Government and Politics, and English Language and Composition were not only excited about the rich content and interactive elements, but they were inspired by the historical documentation provided through the NBC News archives.

NBC had built a better mousetrap and was just waiting for the world to beat a path to its door. In iCue, NBC News perceived that it had a solution for schools, one that would help reinvent learning and would also reinvent NBC News. Despite the challenges encountered by the iCue team in developing and launching its product, by the summer of 2007, it felt that it was far enough along to tell the world about what it had done.

The buildup of iCue began before the 2007 "soft launch" (essentially a limited beta product) and continued until April 2008, when the product would finally officially see the light of day. The first big public showing came a month before Steve Capus's message to the NBC Universal community at the Advanced Placement Teachers' Convention in Las Vegas in July 2007. iCue and the internal unit that it spawned, NBC Learn, still maintained a focus on the AP market, despite the now broader market being pursued for the Archives on Demand, and the team wanted to make a big splash with that AP community.

It is unclear whether AP teachers at that 2007 event were overwhelmed by the product itself or simply by the lavish prelaunch that took place at the convention. In a hall at the Venetian, packed with eight hundred to a thousand teachers and adorned with large screens and elaborate decorations, NBC News showed off its new product to the target audience amidst an open bar, first-class food, and live music. A slick launch video featuring the network's top talent—*NBC Nightly News* anchor Brian Williams, *Meet the Press* fixture Tim Russert, and *The Today Show*'s Meredith Vieira— debuted the product and was followed by a carefully choreographed live demo that went off with only a few small hitches. The affair likely cost $100,000 or more to produce, and in one fell swoop showed how a corporate-backed product was distinct from an academic one.

Even if the teachers were excited about the product itself, the question was, "Did it matter?" As producer Beth Nissen notes:

It cost a fortune and none of these teachers had buying power. These were AP teachers. Now, some of them, because they were AP teachers, the experienced ones—very often an AP teacher will be the head of the department, the head of the English department for that high school—but they didn't have the buying power. That's not who buys this material. They can recommend, they can ask, but it was really kind of money down the drain. . . . Now that we know a lot more about the way schools operate, the way budgets are devised, what kind of lines from budgets we fit into, it's reflected in our pricing models. We know now that with some schools, the only kind of extra money—not spoken for to fix the lighting and the roof in that classroom, or to hire back that teacher you had to let go or furlough over the summer— the only flexible money might be a Teaching American History grant.

So although teachers, maybe even thousands of teachers, could get excited about iCue, the pathway to sales of other services, such as the Archives on Demand, was unclear at best. If the masses arrive at your door and have no purchasing power, it won't matter. The team needed to reach the people with that power. These administrators were not likely the end users of the product and might have little stake in whether the teachers used that product if it didn't align with accountability practices. Furthermore, though a thousand teachers seems like a large crowd, these teachers represented the mavericks and early adopters, the ones who get excited about going to AP conferences and seeing the latest materials. They were not necessarily representative of the larger population.

In Everett Rogers's *Diffusion of Innovations* (2003) model of how innovative processes and products spread through a population, he identifies different groups within a population with respect to their readiness to adopt innovations. Out at the front of the wave are the *innovators*. Innovators have high risk tolerance and are ready to adopt untested innovations, many of which might fail. They represent about 2.5 percent of the population (see figure 8.1). The next wave consists of the *early adopters*, who make

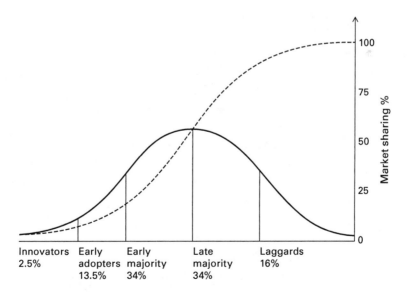

Figure 8.1
Waves of adopters of new innovations as expressed in Everett Rogers's *Diffusion of Innovations* (2003). The innovators who first adopt an innovation are the leading 2.5 percent of the population.

up an additional 13.5 percent of the population. The early adopters are also risk takers, but they adopt innovations after additional evaluation. The early adopters can move fairly rapidly behind the innovators. The *early majority*, representing 34 percent of the population, comes next. What is most notable about the members of this group is that they can take a long time to follow behind the early adopters. (We'll visit other implications of *Diffusion of Innovations* later in this chapter.)

Chisholm had estimated that there were about 615,000 students taking the three relevant AP exams in 2004. (See the breakdown later in this section.) Assuming a student-to-teacher ratio of 20:1, there would be about 30,750 teachers. So the 800 to 1,000 teachers at the AP conference at which NBC News was presenting perhaps represented the innovators and the first wave of early adopters—the leading 2 to 3 percent. There were likely several hundred more teachers in that leading wave who might be innovators or early adopters who were not at the conference, but that audience was going to get tapped out pretty quickly, leaving the next wave of the early majority quite some distance down the road—a road that hadn't even yet been built. The product that the teachers at this event saw was limited in scope. It was likely even too limited to build up momentum within the community until the final product was launched the following year.

Still, these numbers weren't totally off base from some of Chisholm's original projections. During the initial pitch to NBC News, Chisholm had estimated that 615,000 students took the three target AP exams (262,000 in US History, 113,000 in US Government and Politics, and 240,000 in English Literature and Composition). Of those, he had expected to capture 10 to 20 percent in that first year, meaning 26,000 to 52,000 students in US history, or 61,500 to 123,000 students overall. If the mode of reaching these students were through teachers, that would mean 1,300 to 2,600 US history teachers and 3,000 to 6,000 teachers overall (again, assuming about twenty students per teacher). Given these projections, nothing should have quieted the enthusiasm over reaching this AP audience, *except* that the model was built on student use, and it relied completely on these teachers bringing in all of their students. That is a big exception for what was originally conceived of as a student-centered product.

Although some marketing principles would dictate that 20 percent of a market is a rousing success, this audience alone would be inadequate for iCue, resulting in a cost of $5,000 or more per teacher reached. Too much money had been spent, and NBC was relying on iCue to pave a way forward for the network.

Although the Las Vegas launch was big, the fallout afterward was just as big. As visions of the project diverged, deadlines came and went and the price tag continued to grow; what was projected to be a $10 million development passed $15 million early in 2008. As the team packed up and left Las Vegas, the project was a pressure cooker. The seeds were planted for a shakeup—shortly thereafter, senior producer Carol Williams was ousted from the team, and Alex Chisholm left as well (though he did continue to provide advice). As the project evolved, it was clear to Chisholm that the more participatory features of iCue to which he was wedded were going to be marginalized over time in favor of the Archives on Demand, and he was tired of fighting. Their departures may be viewed as the inevitable turnover in management that occurred in the dot-com boom when the visionary founding executives stepped aside to be replaced by others for day-to-day operations, but it was a difficult time for all involved.

The Light of Day

The private growing pains had subsided somewhat by the time of the media blitz accompanying the site's official launch late in the spring of 2008. NBC News did press releases, interviews, and publicity to create some brand awareness and articulate its mission. As this happened, in May 2008, the iCue Advanced Placement courses had yet to see the light of day. The Archives on Demand project was moving along, and the debut version of iCue was focused not on the AP courses but instead on the election- and adult-centered Decision '08 course:

NBC News Launches Safe, Free, Collaborative Online Learning Community Based on MIT Research

iCue Immerses Users in EdutainNet—Education, Entertainment, and Peer Networking

New York, NY—(May 5, 2008)—Today, NBC News unveiled iCue, a pioneering collaborative learning community informed by MIT research that incorporates gaming, discussion and video resources in a fun, safe, online environment. . . .

Designed using research from the MIT Education Arcade (a research group devoted to integrating gaming and peer collaboration into traditional learning activities and environments), iCue offers an unrivaled learning platform—using patented technology of the iCue CueCard—engaging members in authentic, natural learning by incorporating both fun and education in an intuitive, safe, and peer-supported environment.

"*iCue will* forever change the standards for self-directed and communal learning [emphasis added]. *The CueCard technology dramatically alters how video, digital content, and peer networking can be used to support student learning, all within a safe, engaging virtual environment,*" said Steve Capus, President of NBC News. "*iCue not only gives students and lifelong learners a dynamic and content rich experience, it is EdutainNet— education, entertainment, and peer networking.*" . . .

iCue, created by NBC News, is part of a new education initiative dedicated to providing resources to students, teachers, and lifelong learners.

The press release clearly indicates that NBC News believed it had indeed invented the better mousetrap. The notion that iCue would "forever change the standards for self-directed and communal learning," and "dramatically alter" how new technologies would support student learning, was almost absurdly confident. Nevertheless, this sense of a mission, of really moving the needle in education, was unusual coming from a major broadcaster. The language might have been dramatic, but the ideas were consistent with those of education thought leaders. In one interview, Jones pointed out the way in which this new product not only would be important for NBC News, but could fundamentally change the way students learn:

Naturally, the paradigm we are looking at is that, in the classroom right now, it's one student with one teacher: that is the learning relationship. What the power of community says is that a student that goes into a classroom can learn, not only from a teacher, but *can learn from any of the students* within that classroom, or indeed, on the wider scale, [from] students in their school, in their own school district, and perhaps on the other side of the country. Clearly, it's not a question of copying, but it's a question of a student interacting with another student somewhere else, and both of them trying to learn together.

But ultimately, we see this as *a new way of learning* which can be for undergraduate students, for postgraduate, for higher education, for professional development, or even for consumers who just have a natural inclination and understanding for going back over particular areas that interest them. So we think this has a very broad appeal.

[We'll be] having students mark each other's work, and that's part of the *gaming engine within iCue, which is points-based,* and we will be rewarding students for activities that actually encourage the community behavior. So if I submitted homework to you, Elliott, then I would get points for that. You would then get points for rating me, because you are then forced to think about the critical points of my argument that you would support in any exam environment. (Jones, quoted in Masie 2008, emphasis added)

A number of things stand out in this section of the interview. Foremost, Jones sees iCue as shifting the learning model from something teacher-directed (a broadcast model) to one that is peer-based (a network model). One could dismiss this perspective as mere marketing (in light of the language used in the rest of the marketing effort), but this is something that the team was legitimately trying to do: substantially change the learning model to incorporate a practice-based community of learning theorized by social constructivists. iCue was not aimed directly at the end user or learner for sales, but was instead meant to promote collaborative, peer-to-peer learning. The collaborative component of iCue was front and center— everything from community discussions to peer review of work and social networking were integral to the design and helped define iCue.

Jones was also keying in on the idea of awarding points for all of a user's activity in the space. It wouldn't be until a couple of years later that the idea of "gamification" would really take off. Today, we see everything from diet websites to location-based check-in services going the route of gamification. Users are awarded points for checking in, referring friends, viewing entries, and contributing content for many services. Although this idea in many ways trivializes the notion of the deep learning that games can promote, many people believe it does foster participation and commitment to sites. Regardless of the merits of this approach, iCue was a forerunner in this regard.

Although previously Jones had sought to align iCue with textbook publishers to promote the transformative methods that he espoused, by this point he had all but given up on them. Like many lifelong educational technologists, he was lashing out at the conservative textbook industry, bringing forward fairly clear visions of the impact of his technology on the textbook industry. In an interview with *US News and World Report*, Jones said "Video will replace the textbook." He further noted, "Teaching methods have largely remained unchanged for over 100 years." The article also cites Jones's disappointment while searching for a textbook publishing partner for the project, reporting a lack of "common ground" and pointing at the "virtual monopoly" the textbook industry had enjoyed (Lageese 2008). For many like Jones, the textbook industry was the poster child for the status quo in education. Textbooks promote teacher-directed, content-heavy education, which stands in stark contrast to the peer-oriented, twenty-first-century skills-based education promoted in iCue's designs. What was unclear, because of the general unreliability of corporate marketing rhetoric, was whether these words challenging the textbook industry were a call to arms for real change or simply a means to attract educators and learners who had become disenchanted with the slow pace of change.

The "video as textbook replacement" theme struck a note with many people. Blog posts with titles such as "Video, the New Textbook" and "Another Model for Textbooks of the Future?" sprung up in response to the press. Though it may be that the story of video replacing textbooks made for a juicy narrative, it did seem clear that there were many people rooting for textbooks to be toppled. In some ways, though, these posts missed the point. It wasn't the introduction of video into the curriculum that held the most potential as a transformative agent. Instead, it was the way in which the video was being delivered, as part of a collaborative, social, interest-driven site.

The message about iCue's transformative nature was furthered by Steve Capus; a number of news agencies picked up some of his comments:

"At NBC News, we have made a big commitment to working in the education space, and this project is the most substantial one yet," said NBC News President, Steve Capus. "There is tremendous opportunity to combine our vast resources of information with an audience that is hungry for it in an environment they are comfortable consuming it. That, combined with the technology of iCue which dramatically alters how *video, digital content, and peer networking* can be used to support student learning in a safe, engaging virtual environment, makes this an incredibly exciting project." (Greppi 2008)

Capus points to video's content as a significant part of the transformative equation, but he also gives a nod to peer networking and how that supports student learning.

Diffusion of Innovation

The leaders at NBC News felt as if they had an important innovation on their hands, and they tried their hardest to get the word out. Regardless of how novel the final instantiation of iCue was, a significant question to consider was whether this innovation was poised to spread and grow. iCue led a dual life as a product for students and a product for teachers. As a product for students, it led one to think about its ability simply to spread directly from student to student, being used as they saw fit. Considering a product's spread among teachers necessitated not only viewing it as something that teachers might like to adopt, but also factoring in the substantial constraints and special conditions of schools.

As for the student case: understanding that market, and the process by which iCue might be adopted and spread, can be addressed through models of "diffusion of innovation." Although varying models exist to explain such diffusion, Everett Rogers's (2003) model is one of the most well established.

As Rogers describes, there are four main components that are germane to the diffusion of innovations:

1. *Innovation*—The innovation is the "idea, practice or object perceived as new" by the people who are doing the adoption.

2. *Communication Channels*—The communication channels are the means by which people hear about or learn about the innovation.

3. *Time*—Time is important for individuals as they go from knowing about an innovation to actually adopting it, and also for understanding how innovations pass through populations.

4. *Social System*—The social system is the structure in which individuals make decisions regarding the adoption of innovations.

For the most part, the invention of iCue was about the innovation itself—the product is what the leaders emphasized in their press releases and events. What is important here is how iCue was perceived by its audience. It may not matter in the end how much of what iCue offered was entirely new, but the context in which it was applied and the mode by which it was disseminated made it seem new to its audience. In that respect, it was an innovation.

What would influence the adoption of that innovation by the audience were five key characteristics of innovations themselves (Rogers 2003):

1. *Relative advantage* is the degree to which an innovation is perceived as better than the idea it supersedes.

2. *Compatibility* is the degree to which an innovation is perceived as being consistent with the existing values, past experiences, and needs of potential adopters.

3. *Complexity* is the degree to which an innovation is perceived as difficult to understand and to use.

4. *Trialability* is the degree to which an innovation may be experimented with on a limited basis.

5. *Observability* is the degree to which the results of an innovation are visible to others.

The most successful innovations (in terms of adoption) will have a large and immediately perceived relative advantage over previous technologies, will be compatible with the current needs and practices of adopters, will be simple to understand, will be capable of being tested on a limited basis, and will be highly visible to others. A good recent example that satisfies most of these criteria is the innovation of app stores—self-contained, online digital distribution centers for software. App stores offer the *advantage* that they put software in one easy place for people to browse and obtain software at reasonable prices, whereas the previous models—having to go to stores and wade through boxes or find the right website for a particular product—were cumbersome. App stores are *compatible* with the way people have become accustomed to shopping online. One of the immediately obvious advantages that app stores have is their *simplicity*— you click on software and it is downloaded and installed and even provides regular updates. Though some software offers trial versions, the app stores themselves offer *trialability* in their offerings of free software that you can download. And finally, app stores make the process highly social and *visible* via ratings, reviews, and lists of top sellers.

For iCue to be a successful innovation when it was finally released, it would need obvious benefits over other tools and technologies that students use to study for the AP exams. It would also need to not require significant changes in the way the students worked. It would need to be simple to use—a site that a student could log in to and immediately know where to go and what to do. But the student would also need to be able to try it out in small ways and experiment. And finally, when students did things with iCue, that would need to be made known to their peers.

The *communications channels* surrounding iCue might be the most significant and obvious factors that differentiated it from most of the well-studied examples of the diffusion of educational technologies. The events, releases, and marketing as seen here were certainly evidence of that.

However, Rogers makes a distinction between two qualitatively different sources of communication—*mass-media* channels and *interpersonal* channels. iCue had the advantage of ease of access to *mass media*. It *was* mass media. Thus it was easy to distribute the message about iCue to large audiences quickly, which seems like an obvious win. It is worth noting that although such channels enable rapid dissemination of a message, *interpersonal* channels, which support personal and social-networking connections, can be much more influential in determining whether the message about an innovation translates into adoption. This was the mode of communication that NBC News couldn't control.

Perhaps the most important thing to know about the diffusion of an innovation is that it takes *time*—sometimes a lot of time—both for individuals to adopt it and for that adoption to spread from person to person. People need to learn about the innovation and go through a series of stages of experimentation and use before actually adopting it. The innovation needs to spread across the different groups (innovators, early adopters, early majority, late majority, and laggards) that adopt innovations in waves. The earlier groups are small, and the process takes time to reach the larger population. It is noteworthy that such time can be a strong deterrent against innovation within a company that has its eye on the bottom line from day one—one of the reasons that many of the early meetings the Education Arcade had with publishers went nowhere when risk-averse publishers weren't willing to wait for those returns.

Finally, the *social structure* is important when developing educational technologies, as it matters who makes purchasing decisions and how those people make up their minds. For the home market, do parents or students make the decisions? For the school market, is it teachers, department heads, principals, or states? How do these different potential purchasers make up their minds? Ultimately, figuring out this network, and the way in which one might influence it, is critical to the success of an educational technology product.

Diffusion in Schools

If instead of landing directly in the hands of students, iCue were to come through schools and teachers, the previous argument still would hold true. But the process by which innovations are evaluated and adopted for formal instructional practice complicates things further. Roschelle, Tatar, and Kaput (2008) place their study of SimCalc in a framework for diffusion of innovations, specifically for schools. They call upon a model developed by Cohen and Ball (1999) that describes a framework for thinking about scaling up innovations in the classroom.

Cohen and Ball lay out their ideas in an attempt to understand why so few curricular or tool-based interventions in schools have made any difference at all. "Unfortunately, three decades of research has found that *only a few interventions have had detectable effects on instruction and that, when such effects are detected, they rarely are sustained over time*" (1999, 1; emphasis added). Detectable increases in scores and sustained use of iCue would be necessary for iCue to survive. Cohen and Ball offer several explanations for the lack of success of previous efforts, including that schools are complex places and that most professional development inadequately addresses teacher learning. They also lament that most interventions focus on a single factor—the curriculum, or technology—just as iCue was doing. Instead, they propose a model that also adds students and teachers, as well as the interactions of each of these with the other and with the curriculum or technology. Student and teacher experience and expertise can substantially affect how tools and curricula are used and interpreted. Successful interventions, they say, should focus on as many of these interacting pairs as possible.

Groff and Mouza's (2008) i5 framework for teacher adoption of technologies considers these same factors and adds the context of school itself as a fourth factor. This model concerns what teachers might consider as they prepare themselves for using new technologies in teaching. Unfortunately, the nature of all of these interactions, aside from the technology itself, was beyond the scope of expertise at NBC News, which continued to focus on the product. Still, if the product was everything it was touted to be in the press releases, perhaps that would be sufficient to propel it forward. The problem was that the information in those press releases was just *ideas about* the product. It still remained to be seen what the product would be when it saw the light of day.

9 What's Your iCue?

In April 2008, as iCue was nearing launch, the presidential election was in high gear, providing the opportunity to attract a timely audience to that part of the site. But at the same time, the AP season was winding down, with exams scheduled in May. This timing provided poor alignment with the school calendar. Regardless of how well they were aligned, iCue launched with the three AP courses and Election '08. The question was, how did what launched compare to what had been designed at the outset? Looking back, the original purpose of iCue was to:

• Provide access to a vast set of previously unavailable archival materials

• Directly tie archival material to AP course syllabi through browse and search features

• Allow students to explore and play with media through games, blogs, and discussion forums

• Establish a rich "learning community" around the NBC News and partner brands

• Immerse students in a new online educational experience that did not currently exist

Did the product that emerged after years of redesign and negotiation capture these elements? To determine an initial measure of success for iCue's design, we will compare how well the proposed elements of iCue aligned with what actually emerged.

CueCards

So we launched iCue at the end of April 2008 with the four courses in it. We had then obviously built up the social networking features. We had really perfected the

CueCard technology. That was our revolutionary flippable media player, which we absolutely love and anybody who has ever seen it just says, "My god, that is so cool!"

The pride and joy of iCue (evidenced by the above quote from Adam Jones), as well as its central artifact of activity, were the CueCards (see figures 9.1, 9.2, and 9.3). The cards mostly feature clips from the NBC archives and the new NBC materials produced for the site, but some articles from the *New York Times* and the *Washington Post* made it in as well. Alone, this asset met the first of the goals for iCue. The front of the final card contained the media player, with links to notations and content sharing. On the back of the card, users could write their own notes (the "jots" tab) and metadata ("tags"), as well as view producer-groomed metadata ("key-

Figure 9.1
An iCue page for the US Government and Politics course, with one artifact in focus (lower left).

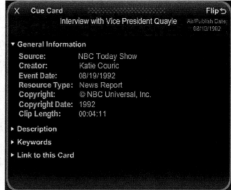

Figure 9.2
The front (left) and back (right) of the CueCard. The front shows fairly standard video controls for the clip, in addition to icons that facilitated sharing of the clip via social media. The back (reached through the Flip button) shows metadata and keywords.

words") and additional information about the content and its origins. In the case of videos, a transcript of the video was provided to improve accessibility and search functions and to allow better integration with traditional written school assignments.

These cards, including any notes or metadata that had been added, could then be shared and collaborated on with other users, allowing them to build connections with "friends" over time. The cards also contained a "comments" section in which users could connect with others and have conversations about the content of the cards. Participants on iCue could "snag" particular CueCards and collect and organize them in "stacks"—sets of related tagged cards that could be regularly referred back to or shared (figure 9.4).

CueCards were the key bridge between the static media of the twentieth century (video clips of news broadcasts) and the more interactive media of today. By empowering users not only to view media, but also to claim them as their own, iCue blended twentieth-century media with twenty-first-century social media consumption and participation.

iCue Pages

The CueCard was a standout success at the time of its release, helping meet the goals for the product. The rest of the goals were tied to the activities

Figure 9.3
The jot function on the front of the CueCard allows users to make their own notes about the video clip.

Figure 9.4
A stack of CueCards collected by a user could be stored and categorized under the user's account.

and materials structured around the CueCards and ultimately relied on the community that would, it was hoped, form around them. As shown in chapter 3, there were ten discrete sections that iCue was to be built around in order to create the online space and accompanying community:

1. Home Page
2. Student Profile Page
3. Game Page
4. Blog Page
5. Daily Questions Page
6. Student Center Pages (including Discussion Boards, IM Tools, Creative Media Tools)
7. Course Syllabi
8. Gaming and Creative Palettes
9. Leader Boards
10. Browse and Search (Advanced)

Some of these made it into the final product, others were modified (sometimes substantially), and some were never there. The story of what happened in iCue and why it happened has much to do with the filter that determined what made it into the final product and how that content looked when it got there.

There was indeed a *home page* (figure 9.5) that aggregated much of the content for each course. It contained a lot of information, including links to activities, a question of the day (discussed later in this section), and quick access to the course outline. It also had a number of tabs that provided access to additional content.

The *student profile* was also present. This page was deeply connected to the social networking aspect of iCue and the notion of friends. The "friends" component of iCue was much like that in other social networking

Figure 9.5
iCue's US Government and Politics course home page, showing Thought Starters (left), Question of the Day (center), and links to games and other parts of the course.

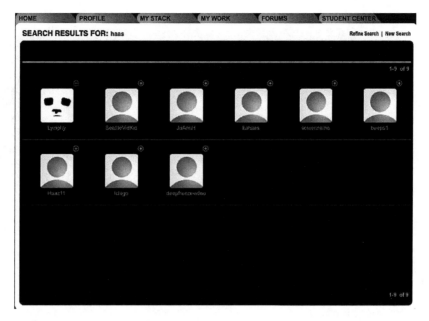

Figure 9.6
Searching for the real names of friends brought up a list that one could browse.

products (e.g., Facebook). You could search lists of people in the system (by their real names or other criteria) and then request friendship with them (figure 9.6).

Once friendship was granted, the friends could see links to one another on their profile pages (figure 9.7). Those links in turn allowed the friends to see one another's profiles. In that way, they could view information about their friends—most notably, the friends' recent work and their stacks. From there, the friends could delve deeper and actually open up the work that their friends had done, promoting social learning. They could view completed games or written activities, to learn from and comment on these pieces of work. What they could not see was much personal information typically associated with social networks. There was no personally identifying information—the best resolution one could get on that was the home state. There was no free-form "wall" in which one could post random thoughts on other people's pages, no photos or other outside media, and no means of getting in contact with any of one's friends. All of these components had been substantially muted based on feedback from teachers during the design process.

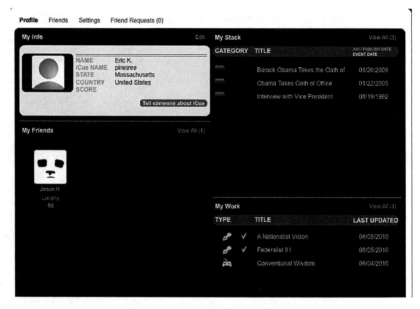

Figure 9.7
The participants' profile pages contained information about them, along with their work, their stacks of media, and their friends.

Despite the limitations, the ability to create a social bond and reputation among users offered a great deal of possibility for learning. iCue's participants would be encouraged to engage with the site's assets, and their progress was documented (figure 9.8). Because this occurred in a social context, players were encouraged to take their work and play seriously; reputation and social connection are powerful motivators. Furthermore, it has been established that being able to coach someone else successfully reflects a deep understanding of the material. The peer-to-peer learning traded on faith in self-directed learning, and subsequently had more appeal in informal learning contexts. Teachers were loath to incorporate these technologies into their classrooms because of the potential additional workload and in some cases the loss of classroom control. "Friending" in this context could have the same flaws it might in many contemporary online social networks (the "Circles" of Google+ are a notable exception)— these friendships were technical binaries (i.e., to the system you either are friends or aren't friends), not an actual measurement of the strength of these relationships, which would permit differential sharing. In the next

Figure 9.8
Friends could delve into and view each other's work.

chapter, we will spend some time examining the importance of the strength of these connections.

The *game page* wasn't so much a page in the end, but a link from the home page of each course under the category "More Activities." The demotion from full-fledged page to an "additional" activity reflected the confidence (or lack thereof) in the NBC News group in producing games that would be of a quality that matched other components of the site. Still, there were three games featured on the home page of each course.

The three games provided for each course were Timeline, Concentration, and Connections (figure 9.9). Each game had three levels of difficulty, increasing the challenge by adding more cards or creating more-difficult conceptual scenarios to complete.

Timeline was about connecting events chronologically. The game started with two CueCards representing a first and a last event. The player was given several CueCards to insert in between these events in the correct order (figure 9.10). The correct order wasn't always obvious from the clips, including those that had stated production dates, which might be off by many years from the event dates. The game was designed to challenge students to contextualize stories that they know relative to one another in time. There were right and wrong answers that could clearly be marked according to the dates of the actual events that were noted in the metadata for each of the CueCards. But one could get more points by putting all of the events in the proper sequence, noting that the relative position of the events might be as important as the actual dates of those events.

Figure 9.9
The three game types that were presented to players: Timeline, Connections, and Concentration. Each course had games based on a particular topic in that course.

Concentration was a twist on a traditional "memory" game that also incorporated categorization skills (figure 9.11). Players were presented with an array of modified CueCards whose "back side" data had been removed and replaced. Each CueCard could be double-clicked to view the video and information on the associated CueCard. Users could also flip the cards over in place to see a category on the back, which was then used to make matches with other CueCards. The matches were not identical, but rather had historical themes or topical connections in common. That theme was revealed in a clue at the bottom of the screen. Like Timeline, Concentration had a familiar style of interaction for players. Although the specifics of basing the games on the interactive video cards, and the particular categorization, were unique, the game itself was familiar. This design had the positive effect of providing a shallow on-ramp to these two games.

Connections was the final implementation of Chisholm's Dominoes game. The game as realized was remarkably faithful to his original design (figure 9.12). As in Concentration, the players' cards were modified to

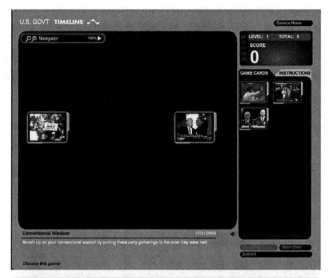

Figure 9.10
A Timeline game showing the original configuration with two CueCards representing beginning and end, along with CueCards to be inserted in between (above) and the final timeline with all media in place, showing the chronological links among the events (below).

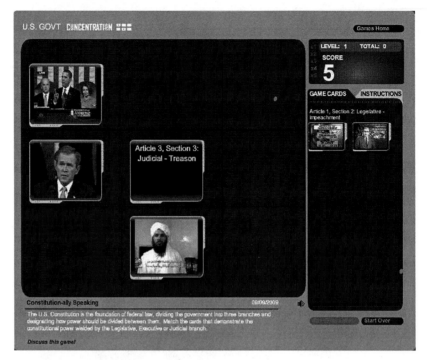

Figure 9.11
A round of Concentration shows matches of CueCards already paired (in the right-hand column) along with CueCards still in play (one of them turned over to display category information).

increase the game's challenge. CueCards with common keywords could be linked to one another. The game then used the producer-created keywords to make the connections among events. The players' scores were determined by the number of connections they create when they put each card onto the playing board for the first time. Users were essentially "writing" a narrative by linking these shorter narratives into a complicated web, coming to an understanding about unexpected connections that undergird our history and our politics. This game was the least familiar to players entering the iCue space, which also meant it was the most innovative. It borrowed the notion of network graphs that players might have seen (e.g., visualizations of social networks) but likely hadn't interacted with. The gameplay, however, turned out to be a challenge to program flexibly. Although the game gives an impression of nearly unlimited connection

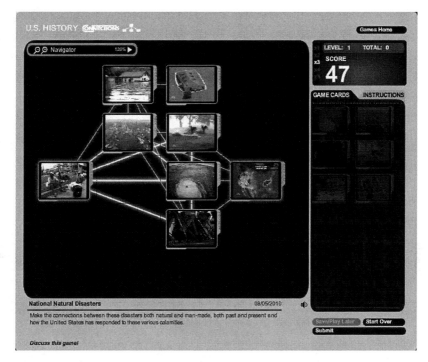

Figure 9.12
A Connections game, which starts with Hurricane Katrina and ends with forecasts of record drought. CueCards are used to connect the events in between. In this case, many of the events have connections to many of the other events.

possibilities, it actually is quite constrained to make particular connections based on keywords. At best, this eliminates much of the creative thinking that players might use to devise new and unique connections, and more likely made the activity into something in which the player was simply guessing the connections the designers had in mind.

The *blog page* was not a traditional blog (if such a thing even exists). A space to express freely whatever was on one's mind would not have worked for teachers, who expressed reservations about such unfettered student expression in the academic space. Instead, the blogs took the form of the *Writing Challenges* (figures 9.13 and 9.14), which were designed based on the AP tests' DBQ essays. A Writing Challenge provided several stories on CueCards as primary documents and a question related to those media clips, licensed from the College Board's actual AP questions. The users

Figure 9.13

A Writing Challenge that shows the question, along with a timer, workspace, and relevant CueCards.

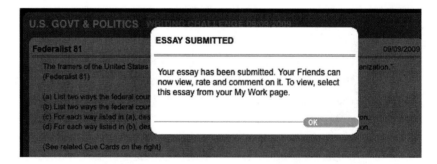

Figure 9.14

Once Writing Challenges were submitted (left) they could be read, rated, and commented on by participants' friends.

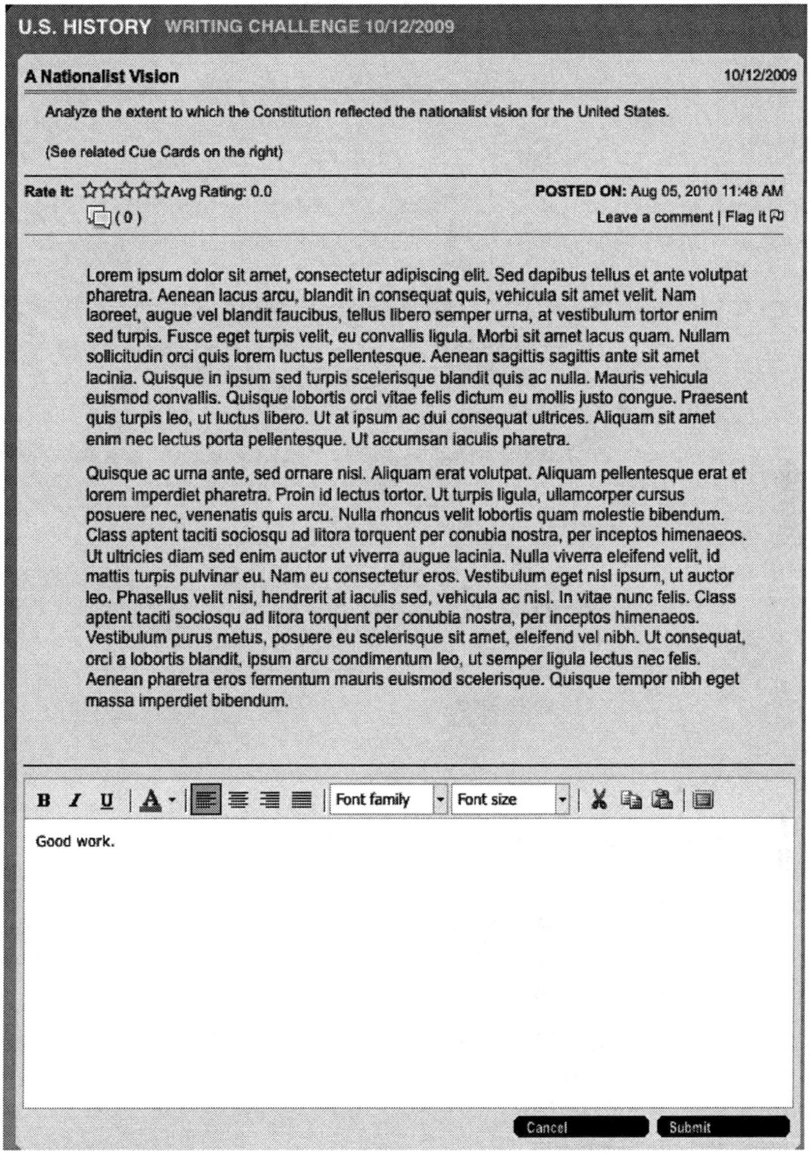

U.S. HISTORY WRITING CHALLENGE 10/12/2009

A Nationalist Vision 10/12/2009

Analyze the extent to which the Constitution reflected the nationalist vision for the United States.

(See related Cue Cards on the right)

Rate it: ☆☆☆☆☆Avg Rating: 0.0   POSTED ON: Aug 05, 2010 11:48 AM

💬(0)   Leave a comment | Flag it 🏳

Lorem ipsum dolor sit amet, consectetur adipiscing elit. Sed dapibus tellus et ante volutpat pharetra. Aenean lacus arcu, blandit in consequat quis, vehicula sit amet velit. Nam laoreet, augue vel blandit faucibus, tellus libero semper urna, at vestibulum tortor enim sed turpis. Fusce eget turpis velit, eu convallis ligula. Morbi sit amet lacus quam. Nullam sollicitudin orci quis lorem luctus pellentesque. Aenean sagittis sagittis ante sit amet lacinia. Quisque in ipsum sed turpis scelerisque blandit quis ac nulla. Mauris vehicula euismod convallis. Quisque lobortis orci vitae felis dictum eu mollis justo congue. Praesent quis turpis leo, ut luctus libero. Ut at ipsum ac dui consequat ultrices. Aliquam sit amet enim nec lectus porta pellentesque. Ut accumsan iaculis pharetra.

Quisque ac urna ante, sed ornare nisl. Aliquam erat volutpat. Aliquam pellentesque erat et lorem imperdiet pharetra. Proin id lectus tortor. Ut turpis ligula, ullamcorper cursus posuere nec, venenatis quis arcu. Nulla rhoncus velit lobortis quam molestie bibendum. Class aptent taciti sociosqu ad litora torquent per conubia nostra, per inceptos himenaeos. Ut ultricies diam sed enim auctor ut viverra augue lacinia. Nulla viverra eleifend velit, id mattis turpis pulvinar eu. Nam eu consectetur eros. Vestibulum eget nisl ipsum, ut auctor leo. Phasellus velit nisi, hendrerit at iaculis sed, vehicula ac nisl. In vitae nunc felis. Class aptent taciti sociosqu ad litora torquent per conubia nostra, per inceptos himenaeos. Vestibulum purus metus, posuere eu scelerisque sit amet, eleifend vel nibh. Ut consequat, orci a lobortis blandit, ipsum arcu condimentum leo, ut semper ligula lectus nec felis. Aenean pharetra eros fermentum mauris euismod scelerisque. Quisque tempor nibh eget massa imperdiet bibendum.

B *I* <u>U</u> | **A** ▾ | ▤ ≣ ≣ ≣ | Font family ▾ | Font size ▾ | ✂ 🗐 📋 | ▣

Good work.

Cancel   Submit

Figure 9.14

(continued)

could then craft an essay in a large text window. They could time themselves and save drafts, allowing them to practice in conditions similar to an actual AP exam while giving them control over their practice conditions. Saved essays were preserved for future work and "submitted" essays were viewable by the participant's "friends" on the site, who could rate and comment on the work. The goal was to create a community of practice around writing skills for DBQs.

The *daily questions page* ultimately took over most of the home page, including an open-ended Thought Starter question (a short, pithy current-events piece designed to provoke discussion) and a Question of the Day (practice for the AP exam and regular exposure to relevant content through multiple-choice questions). These materials, along with the Writing Challenge, made up most of the screen real estate as well as the conceptual emphasis on the site, which was initially updated and added to frequently. As Jones recalls about the launch:

At that point we were updating the content on iCue on pretty much daily basis. We were creating daily thought starters. We were basically following the AP curriculum on a weekly basis, so every time you went to iCue on any one of the courses it was serving up content that was relevant to that week's instruction. We decided to license a large bank of past exam questions from the College Board so that on a daily basis you had . . . questions that would actually reinforce instruction. So we were trying to make sure that it was pedagogically sound, that we were really mapping into a curriculum and it was going to be learning based.

The *Thought Starters* appeared dominantly on each course's home page and were links to cards, contextualized around a central question, and connected to a discussion board based on the topic in the video. The link to the discussion boards made this activity in practice perhaps the most social of all of the iCue activities. In the example in figure 9.5, the Thought Starter for the US Government and Politics course is the topic of President Obama's Cabinet picks. Clicking on the "discuss" link would take the users to a discussion board where they could read and offer up their own comments on the topic. The discussion took place in a typical bulletin board system on which participants could respond to the Thought Starter itself, respond to other participants, and also develop reputations for continued responses (figure 9.15).

The multiple-choice questions came in the form of Questions of the Day, also appearing on the course's home page (figure 9.5). These were AP exam–

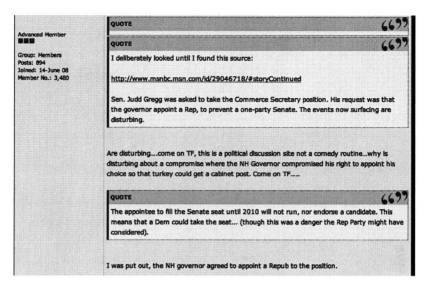

Figure 9.15
The discussion about a Thought Starter shows responses to the Thought Starter as well as responses to other participants' comments.

style questions (some licensed from the College Board, resulting in payments to, instead of from, this organization), drawing both from current events and from the curriculum outlined on the course's home page. Despite being interactive, the Question of the Day was not meant to be particularly challenging. It functioned more to ease the students into the site in a low-stakes way while still connecting them with topic-appropriate content. When users answered the questions, they got immediate feedback on their choices in order to help students learn both what the best answers were and why the other answers were not a better fit.

The *student center pages* were vastly trimmed. There was a link to the Forums, which contained discussions about the Thought Starter questions, in its own tab. What was left for the student center was some topical questions related to current events and stories "of interest" to students. There was some well-curated information there, but it was almost entirely devoid of participatory elements for students.

The *course syllabi* were displayed quite prominently on the home page. They made it abundantly clear that this was a site for the AP exam, which made it easy both to access and to relate to the curriculum, but it also clarified that this was not an open-ended, participatory space. The *gaming* elements were all moved to the "more activities" section, and any *creative* elements that were in the original designs or proposed through the journalism competition were scrubbed entirely. Leader Boards, another social element, were also scrapped from iCue's implementation, but there were (thanks to the extensive metadata) reasonable abilities to *search and browse* CueCards.

iCue Design Alignment and Departure

When iCue launched with all of these components, at first glance it seemed as if it had captured much of the original vision—original video content delivered in an innovative format, social networking with the ability to friend others, materials integrated into interactive games, and direct connections to testing materials. On a simple checklist basis, it had seven of the ten original elements in some form, as well as the major backbone resting on the CueCards. Not a perfect fit, but a reasonable start. However, upon closer inspection, many of those components that were present fell short of their intended purposes.

Most prominently, the system of friending was quite limited. Although you could search and friend others, the process felt constrained and academic. It lacked much of what would be associated with personal social networks—including sharing, posting, and communicating. Additionally, the friending interface was a bit complex, dampening one's interest in friending others. Other parts of what participants did were disconnected from their friends networks, such as posts on Thought Starters. So though social networking was there, it hadn't captured much of the spirit of the social networking sites that many people had already joined. The social gap extended to other elements of the site such as the missing leader boards, leaving participants somewhat isolated within the site.

The other big gap was in the games. The team was originally guided by the designs of Chisholm and advice from the Education Arcade, but in the end the games had constrained budgets and were developed after Chisholm had left by a technical staff that knew little about game design. No one in the organization was in charge of overseeing the games' design or quality. As Jones admits:

I think the team built the games in iCue, but were really uncomfortable . . . they didn't think that they had the expertise to put the framework together and have a real sense of what the games were meant to be. Are they meant to be purely fun and a way of engaging the resource? Or are they meant to be linked to learning outcome and there has to be a check the box at the end—"Have you learned xyz by playing this game?" So there was some anxiety about whether we had the capability to do that, but we did the experimentation.

The games suffered from both the identity crisis that Jones mentions here and interface issues. Despite being innovative in their incorporation of video, they were often cumbersome in the ways in which users interacted with them. They didn't offer the kinds of simple usability or designed feedback that make games an enjoyable interactive experience. One might place a CueCard in a Connections game and not really understand why it made the connections it did or why those broke when you moved the card a bit. NBC, it should be said, was still ahead of a number of learning-games companies, trying to offer games of real substance—it wasn't content to settle for simple vocabulary games. The constructivist ideas were there in the final game, but it was questionable whether they were particularly fun or engaging.

As a learning games organization trying to move the field forward through high-quality games, we found ourselves frustrated and unable to stop what happened with the games. By the third year of our research contract, when iCue was being launched, the iCue team was firmly committed to get into schools and thereby reconfigured what it wanted from the MIT team. It was convinced that it would need incontrovertible proof of iCue's impact on learning, so it asked TEA to step into an evaluative role. In order to be ethical evaluators, the group had divested itself from commenting on the product in the meantime, creating an uncomfortable situation for all. The production machine in Studio 3B was working full tilt to meet deadlines, and all of the designs for games and activities were set in stone. With the shift in their roles from collaborators to evaluators, at this point all the members of TEA could do was sit on their hands, waiting for the site to go live so they could actually get some data. TEA had presented to the iCue team design philosophies and principles as much as we felt was ethical, including in a daylong workshop, but it proved to be too little, too late.

The resulting social networking and games "lite" versions that emerged, combined with the prominence of the AP syllabus and associated AP questions, made the site feel notably less participatory than it had been in the original design, or for that matter in the stated goals of the NBC News team. Although it maintained the façade of new modes of learning, ultimately what differentiated iCue from traditional test prep and learning materials was the CueCards themselves. This issue was exacerbated by what was perhaps the biggest challenge iCue faced in implementation: content. The materials present on the site offered limited use and replayability. In order for the site to be successful, it needed to have regularly updated content that participants would keep coming back for. Those updates occurred regularly at first, done by the large production staff that worked in the division. However, all of that changed when there were cutbacks and reorganization. This reduction put pressure on Jones to make a choice between being CFO and advancing his vision of education. Despite his success with the bottom line for NBC News, he felt stretched between his two commitments, and that was evident to other executives within the organization. Jones explains:

I decided I would commit to making this work. I would hang up my finance boots because I didn't see myself being [there] long term. I thought there was significant value in doing this. I have absolutely no regrets for doing that, but the one thing that did happen immediately was, the moment I was no longer CFO, I no longer was able to incubate this and protect it financially. And the moment that happened, it got bullseyes put all over it. The natural tendency in the organization is to mitigate businesses that are losing money, even if they all have significant strategic importance. So basically, they were trying to shut it down. I ended up having to lay off 75 percent of the workforce on the production team, so it was brutal. That team that was originally sixty is now probably twelve.

And the consequences of that reduction were immediately obvious:

"You can't produce any more content. You can't do any more development. And you can't do anything on marketing, in order to cut costs." Well then, you're almost putting a bullet in it, because if I can't produce content, that's what we do. I can't develop technology and I can't market it, but I really had no choice. It was that or it would be shut down. So I kind of said, OK. We'll do that.

Conclusion

At launch, then, iCue had a number of things going for it. It was reviewed favorably, for the most part, and was noted for its innovations. Anyone who saw a CueCard was amazed and excited. Most teachers instantaneously "got it," especially upon seeing particularly momentous archival footage of moments such as the struggle for civil rights in the 1950s. There was a lot to do on the site, with a feature set for every kind of user.

But it was launched for a mass market, pitched to an indiscriminately large audience (certainly not just to teens). It was loaded with features that were specifically geared to the features of Advanced Placement classes, including the class outlines for three of the released courses, and the Writing Challenges that were derived from the College Board's DBQs. Critics identified the producer-created game challenges and Thought Starters as a central strength of the site, but the substantial cutbacks essentially prohibited content development, as well as marketing and additional technical development. iCue was also launched for free (at least for the testing phase). This decision lowered the barrier to testing it out and even adopting it but provided a premium service without a revenue model. It also meant that iCue was launched and within six months was not maintained as well as it should have been. And the site was perhaps labyrinthine and overstuffed. The social networking was significantly hobbled. This was a product to be proud of, but ultimately not the product that anyone at NBC News or MIT would have preferred to see make it to market. The forces that arise when providing media and technology, particularly innovations, for education had made a mess of things.

What would this mean for adoption of iCue? Cohen and Ball (1999) highlight a tension between the specificity and the flexibility of an intervention. Tightly specified interventions leave less for teachers to have to develop on their own, which they argue increases the probability of follow-through. However, such specificity can greatly increase the cost of development of a product, and may alienate some teachers who either decide they don't like some part of the prescriptive plan or simply don't like curricula that are overly prescriptive. From the perspective of a designer, the latter, less well specified approach, despite reducing costs, also leaves open a wide range of uses that may actually be significant departures from what the designer intended. Ultimately, iCue shaped up to be much more on the flexible side. It was envisioned that a teacher could use just one component or many. A student could meticulously complete all of the activities each week or just come to play a particular game.

Existing on the flexible end of the spectrum allowed for the greatest range of possibilities, but also left iCue open to marginalization. As Cohen and Ball note:

From the enactors' perspective, the default option has been to marginalize—that is, to use the resources that interventions bring while retaining the core of operations unchanged. This strategy requires the least learning and change and has worked very well in U.S. education. Marginalizing interventions keeps the ratio between costs and benefits of enactment in a manageable range and enables enactors to innovate and improve without basic change. In the typical U.S. instructional environment, it is entirely rational. From the typical enactor's perspective, the preferred relationship with intervenors keeps things loose and permissive, with intervenors supplying resources and enactors deciding how to use them. (1999, 25)

What this meant for iCue was that regardless of how transformative it could be for teaching and learning practices, when released into the wild it faced the prospects of users simply adopting the components that fit with existing practice and discarding whatever didn't fit.

Meanwhile, the MIT team was ready to see how people responded to its ideas (even if they were diminished in the final product) in practice. During the press push, Henry Jenkins was quoted in the iCue press release (Nagel 2008) as saying, "The new media literacies are social skills and cultural competencies which young people are acquiring informally through their engagement with games and other virtual playgrounds." He continues: "Young people are putting their heads together, comparing notes, pooling knowledge, and tackling problems collectively that they would not be able to master individually," but we were ready to see some of that learning in action, at sizeable scale. The press was obviously exciting, but it would be important to see what iCue actually was and how it was used. Educational revolutions require active participation and engagement on many levels, and it was unclear whether teachers, administrators, teens, or parents would take to the offering, because of or in spite of its revolutionary promises.

Idealized Experience

With all of the caveats associated with the reality of what iCue turned out to be, there was still a vision of the interesting possibilities of what a student in the space of iCue could do. To give a sense of the activities, and the possibilities that they suggested in the heads of the designers, we will explore an idealized day of use by one user in one subject. (Although users were free to switch from activity to activity or subject to subject at any time, our user will perform all activities in one subject to completion.)

After logging in and heading to the US History course (figure 10.1), the user sees the US History course page depicted in the previous chapter. In the top left corner is the day's Thought Starter, a story about Betty Ford's personal struggle with breast cancer. The caption reads "When First Lady Betty Ford underwent an operation for breast cancer this week in 1974, she helped the nation understand more about a disease that affects hundreds of thousands of women in America." She can then click on the play button and view a CueCard of a report from October 1, 1974, on the increase in the number of women seeking mammograms in the wake of First Lady Ford's surgery. After viewing the video, she can then move into the forums to discuss this topic, where an administrator elaborates on the topic and asks whether users believe men's health issues receive more attention than those of women.

After contributing to the discussion, the user moves back to the US History course page and addresses the Question of the Day, a multiple-choice section. The question says:

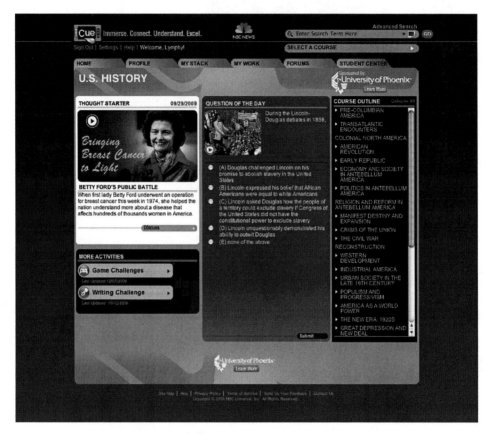

Figure 10.1
The home page for the US History course in iCue, showing the Thought Starter (left), Question of the Day (center), Syllabus (right), and links to Games and Writing Challenges (lower left).

The annexation of Texas

(A) was opposed by many Northerners who disliked the idea of annexing a large slave territory

(B) gained some support as a just act of the nation's manifest destiny

(C) was opposed by Northerners who were threatened by the increase in the number of Southern votes in both Congress and the Electoral College

(D) succeeded when Congress approved the annexation by a joint resolution

(E) All of the above.

The user clicks "D" because she knows this is true from her AP classes; however, the correct answer is "E," all of the above. This correction is expressed to the user via an "X" next to the wrong answer she selected and a check mark next to the correct one.

The user progresses to the Game Challenges. On the Game Challenges page, she chooses to play Connections, this particular instance of which is titled, "Whose Right?"

Upon starting the game, the player has two CueCard stories on either side of the playing space (see figure 10.2). The user investigates the story on the left, about James Madison's desire for a bill of rights, and the story on the right, about artists protesting a ban on cadmium paint because they favor the rich colors cadmium paint allows. In the box on the right, she has six news stories she can use to make a connection between these two stories. The stories are: "FCC Acts to Restrict Indecent Programming," "A Look Back at the Tinker Trial," "California Sets Pace on Environmental Regulation," "Sherriff Recalled over Second Amendment Debate," "75th Anniversary of Women's Right to Vote," and "Bill Grants Students Permission for Religious Clubs." All of these stories have connections to the rights of citizens, so she arranges them on the palette in the manner that she thinks best. The computer measures the relative "strength" of the user's positioning based on the number of producer-chosen keywords the cards have in common (indicated to the user by the thickness of the connecting line) and then awards the user points. When she is satisfied with the positioning of these stories and the narrative that she has told, mixing these narratives in order to tell a story about the relationship between the Bill of Rights and a cadmium paint ban, she submits the game for points. In figure 10.3, the relationship between more clear-cut Bill of Rights issues (such as free speech and concealed-gun licenses) and fuzzier ones such as those complicated by environmental or public safety issues (car emissions and cadmium paint) is made clear—there are many stories that cluster easily around the Bill of Rights, but the stories in which public safety and environmentalism trumped total freedom end up more or less isolated from things more clearly described in the Bill of Rights.

Our user, having completed and submitted her game challenge, returns to the US History course page and heads to the Writing Challenge. The question in this particular Writing Challenge is "Analyze the extent to which the Constitution reflected the nationalist vision for the United States." The user views the clips in the CueCards on the right: "Anniversary of the Signing of the Constitution," in which Katie Couric interviews

Figure 10.2
The Connections game at the beginning (left) and end (right).

Lynne Cheney about a celebration of the Constitution in 2002; "Constitutional Convention Debates" from 1987, in which John Hart takes a look back at the debates that occurred during the convention; and "Constitutional Convention: Big States vs. Small States," also from 1987, in which Jane Pauley talks to then Pennsylvania and Delaware governors Robert Casey and Michael Castle about the historical differences of opinion between their states during the Constitutional Convention. After viewing these clips, the user refers to them in an essay that makes a cogent point about the nationalist perspective in the US Constitution. Because of an upcoming AP test, she decides to use the timer function to time herself for practice. She then saves the essay instead of submitting it (sending it to peers for review) so that she can go back through it to proofread it later.

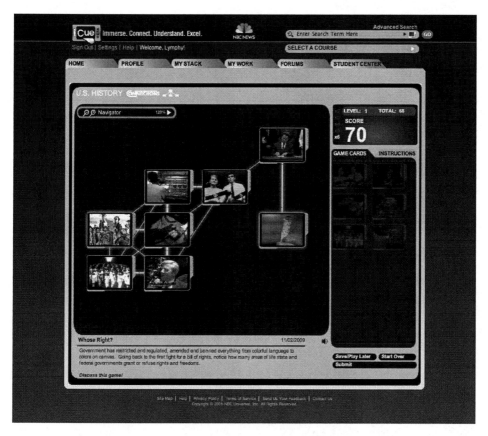

Figure 10.2
(continued)

Before leaving iCue, the user returns to the US History course page one last time to investigate the Course Outline on the right side of the page. The user is studying new urbanism in the nineteenth century, so she clicks on "Industrial America" in the outline and then "Urban Society in the Late 19th Century." She is brought to a page that has all of the stories in iCue that relate to the topic. The user can now dig into this pile, potentially looking for resources for an upcoming term paper.

The Reality Gap

The example experience is quite rich. But when real users—students, teachers, and reviewers—got their hands on the site, iCue's lack of focus

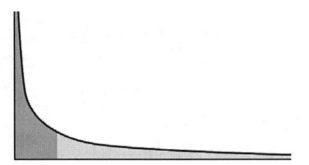

Figure 10.3
A sample power law distribution, where the x axis is some measure (such as time spent on a website) and the y axis is the number of people doing the activity at that frequency.
Source: http://en.wikipedia.org/wiki/power_law.

became apparent. Attempting to head off some of that confusion, NBC News published some information in the iCue Frequently Asked Questions (FAQ) on its website: "It is not a "test prep" program full of boring study drills, and it is not an "edutainment" site full of flashy games but little actual learning. In iCue, YOU—the learner—are in control of how you want to learn, how much time you want to spend, and the activities in which you want to participate." Although this is a learner-centered and progressive message, it does more to establish what iCue is *not* than what it *is*. An early reviewer on CNET noted, "There's a whole lot going on, and I'm betting the casual user is going to get lost very easily." But the same reviewer further noted, "Another thing NBC has definitely gotten right is the video player. Each clip is housed in a tiny floating window that can be flipped over like widgets in OS X's Dashboard. This B-side contains the video's metadata, including an entire set of keywords that pull up a listing of related clips." The closing note in this review was also telling: "NBC's greatest asset is in some of the premade sets of exercises and games, which put the grunt work on the editors instead of the users." In other words, the games and activities were a valuable asset, but the willingness of online communities to contribute and participate was an open question. Furthermore, those valuable assets, created and curated by the iCue team, were an expensive proposition—part of the reason the price tag had already blown through the $15 million mark before most of the real content had gone to market.

The elements were still there for a rich experience, but the data generated by iCue shows that the realized experience captured by our research study was quite different. Our research study of iCue started out as an intensive effort that was to include online usage data, AP scores, and classroom-level detail. As iCue's resources diminished and the scale of classroom usage became somewhat apparent, the bulk of the research shifted its focus to analyses of online datasets. When users signed up for accounts on iCue, they were given the opportunity to opt in to an MIT research study. For those users who opted in, we were able to track all of their activity (keeping the users anonymous) in order to get glimpses of usage patterns and to begin to understand what people were doing on iCue. This kind of data is often difficult or impossible to get from commercial websites. Most other studies have had to rely on reverse engineering from publicly accessible data or traffic sniffing on public networks, so these data could provide some unique insights. The idea was to inform NBC News about what its users were doing, and to investigate the site to see whether we could discover examples of the participatory learning theorized and described by the New Media Literacies group. That was not exactly what we found.

Who Showed Up

NBC News provided us with two similar sets of data, an initial one from August 2008 through the end of 2008, and another that captured the data on spring usage in 2009, which was analyzed by research partners, James K. L. Hammerman and Candy Miller. In all, there were 5,665 users, of which 1,918 (33.9 percent) opted into our study. Users told us a little bit about themselves and allowed us to look at records of their activities on the site. This information included such things as the number of times the users logged into iCue, as well as increasingly detailed information on how many videos they watched at least halfway through or the number of games they "submitted" for others to view. The analysis that follows will, we hope, illuminate just what people did on the site, often in contrast to expectations.

Typical of Internet usage patterns, most of our measures in the study, we found, were highly skewed, in a "power law" or "long-tailed" distribution (Adamic and Huberman 2002; Shirky 2003) (figure 10.5), meaning that there were many people participating a little and a few participating to a much greater extent. For instance, a large number of people logged in to their user accounts at least a few times, but only a small number of users logged in a great deal. This same distribution has been found on social networks such as MySpace (Gyarmati and Trinh 2010) or Orkut and Linke-dIn (Benevenuto et al. 2009), to which a small number of people log in frequently and many people log in just occasionally.

Who Used iCue, and for How Long?

The target audience for iCue was initially high school students, but as we related, NBC ultimately tried to reach this audience through their teachers, as well as the teachers themselves. iCue users were, over all, older than expected. People reported ages from fourteen to ninety-two years with a median age of forty-two.

Users of iCue were quite well educated (figure 10.4). Most reported having master's degrees or higher, and almost a third reported bachelor's degrees. Of the remaining group, a little more than half were high school

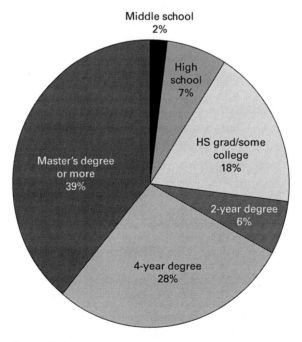

Figure 10.4
Participants by educational level. This chart shows that most users indicate some level of higher education. The few who do not are suspected of indicating the grade that they teach, not their own level of education.

grads, most of whom had some college experience. About equal numbers were in high school or had two-year degrees, and a few were in middle school. The users were relatively evenly split by gender.

If those who provided demographic information for our study accurately reflect the age and educational level of all users of iCue, then iCue did not attract its target audience. iCue was not only reaching a portion of the population that is comfortable with the Internet—those ages eighteen to forty-four who have come of age with the Internet—but was also reaching younger baby boomers who have less comfort with the Internet (Jones and Fox 2009). Furthermore, there were aberrations in the age data that suggest reasons to doubt the age reporting of some allegedly middle school or high school students. In the larger April 2009 demographic data set, the average age for those reporting they were in middle school was thirty-three and a half; the average age for those reporting they were in high school was twenty-eight. We suspect almost all of these people were *teachers* of children of those grades, rather than children who were in those grades themselves. Users may have been selecting the school level at which they taught from a dropdown menu, not the level of schooling they themselves had attained. These oddities cause us to speculate that iCue attracted a large number of educators who themselves had high levels of education (with advanced degrees required for teaching, information technology, or administration). If iCue was attracting teachers, and not the targeted teens, it is worth considering how and where the site was marketed.

The Challenge of Conducting Research Online

It is possible that our numbers might also have skewed older due to the labyrinthine process that young people had to go through in order to agree to participate in our research. The stipulations of the US Children's Online Privacy Protection Act (COPPA) and the MIT Internal Review Board (which approves research projects based on safety and ethical standards) proved to be difficult to navigate (figure 10.5). In the end, young people had to agree to participate in the research themselves as well as provide an email address for parents or guardians who could also approve their participation. Although these regulations and regulatory bodies create important protections for children, in cases such as this, they aren't well adapted for research in online educational technologies. Many colleagues and partners have lamented that similar circumstances suggest the need to improve the ease and opportunities for researchers to have safe access to the online patterns and activities of young people in order to fuel better policy and understandings.

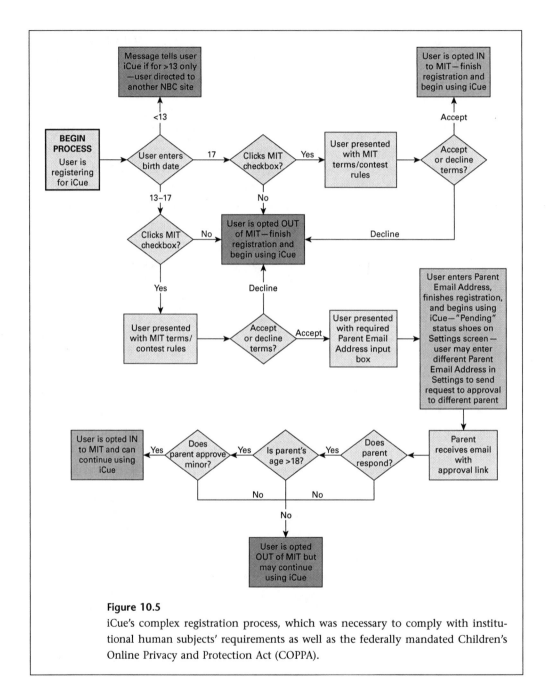

Figure 10.5
iCue's complex registration process, which was necessary to comply with institutional human subjects' requirements as well as the federally mandated Children's Online Privacy and Protection Act (COPPA).

For the audience that did opt in to our study, participation on the site varied by month, with interest peaking in the second month of study, September, when school was starting back up, and then tapering off (see figure 10.6). To explore whether iCue captured people's attention over time, we looked at whether users just tried it for a month and then dropped out, or stuck with it for several months. A large majority of users logged in for only one month. As many of the users in this community were likely pioneers, they tried the site and quickly moved on if they didn't like it. Others have found similar patterns in social networks (Gyarmati and Trinh 2010), although the drop here seems to be more precipitous than that seen elsewhere. Still, about a third of the users in October through December were on the site for two or more months, showing that there was a group of settlers that stuck with the site for some time (figure 10.6).

After looking at how long in months people stayed on the site, we examined the relationship between the amount of time spent on iCue and the number of times a user logged in (figure 10.7). Those who participated on iCue for only one month logged in substantially less, even on a per-month

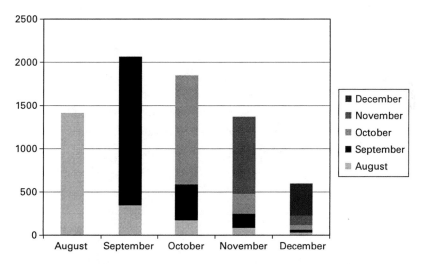

Figure 10.6
Total number of logins by starting month. Following one of the bars across months shows that many of the users who sign up in any given month do not continue into the next month. For example, although nearly 1,500 users started in August, by September fewer than 500 of those users remained (shown in the bottom bar for September). *Note:* December values are for 23 days only.

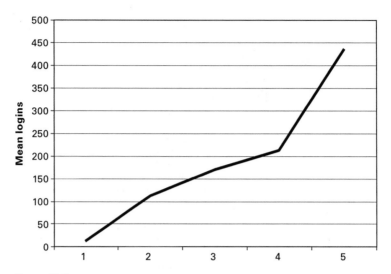

Figure 10.7
Total number of logins by months on iCue. The number of times users log in per month goes up for each month the person has been a member of iCue. This increase is statistically significant only from months one to two. After that the variation in logging in is too great to show a sustained trend. 1 month, $n = 4570$; 2 months, $n = 710$; 3 months, $n = 269$; 4 months, $n = 80$; 5 months, $n = 36$.

basis, than those who participated for two or more months, and statistical tests confirm this. Although the average number of logins continued to increase for people who had logged on for more than two months, the variation in those logins was so high that we couldn't tell if people who logged on for three, four, or five months did so any more frequently than those who were on for just two months.

What Do People Do Once They Get There?

The study looked at the particular activities in which people engaged while on the iCue site. Based on the data that we were able to capture, we broke those activities down into the following categories: *Number of CueCards Opened, Number of Friends, Number of Videos Started, Video Content Seconds Watched, Videos Completed, Number of Games Played, Time Spent on Games,* and *Number of Games Submitted.*

We did not analyze postings in the forums or other writings, even though we had originally intended to do so, because they were used so infrequently that analysis couldn't really tell us anything about them. Forums were used by perhaps only dozens of people, and even then only sporadically. Also, recall that participation on the site in almost all activity areas had a highly skewed (long-tail) distribution, indicating that some people engaged in those activities a lot and that a lot of people engaged in those activities much less. Table 10.1 shows the percentage of people who did the activities, along with the minimum, maximum, and median value for that activity across the 144 days of the analysis.

It's clear from table 10.1 and figure 10.8 that most people (95 percent) were making friends on the site, about half were opening CueCards and watching video, and about a third were playing games. Even though these activities were done by large chunks of the population, they were not done much. The median Number of CueCards Opened for the 55 percent who *did* open them was just five cards; the median Number of Videos Started for the 45 percent who started *any* videos was four; the median Number of Games Played for the 31 percent who played *any* games was just two. These rates indicate that among the activities that were central to the design of iCue, participation was quite low. Still, half the participants

Table 10.1
iCue Activities: Minimum, Maximum, and Median Times for Which Activities Were Done

Activity	% Done	Min	Median	Max
Logins	100	1	17	1742
Friends	95	1	11	1010
CueCards Opened	55	1	5	438
Videos Started	45	1	4	212
Videos Completed	31	1	4	177
Video Content Watched (H:)M:S	45	0:00	5:22	10:15:02
Total Games Played	31	1	2	96
Total Games Submitted	22	1	3	312
Time Spent on Games (H:)M:S	31	0:00	3:18	5:28:51

Note: This table shows the percentage of participants who participated in each activity and the minimum, median, and maximum number of times that a person participated in those activities. The great variability in usage of activities (from making friends at 95 percent to submitting games at 22 percent) and usage within activities (for example opening CueCards, which had a median of five cards per person, but had at least one person who opened 438 cards) is seen here.

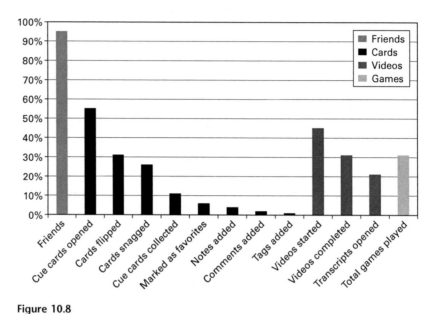

Figure 10.8
Activities by percentage of the population participating. This representation graphically shows the variability in participation across activities, from making friends (at
nearly 100 percent) to adding tags to CueCards, which was done by just a few
percent of the people who came to iCue.

(more than 2,800) were logging on at a rate of once a week or more, and
10 percent of participants (more than 500) were logging on to iCue at a
rate of once a day or more.

Some other interesting issues of engagement emerge from a closer look
at the numbers. When people started watching a video (these were about
three to five minutes long), they finished watching it only 43 percent of
the time. This percentage indicates that users may not have been highly
engaged by the videos, or that perhaps viewers felt they could get the gist
of a story from only part of the video. The games also had issues of engagement. Of the total Number of Games Played, 42 percent were Concentration games, 37 percent were Timeline games, and 21 percent were
Connections games. However, participants *submitted* Concentration games
much more often (64 percent of all games submitted) than they submitted
results from Connections games (11 percent of all games submitted).[4] This

---

4. That is, committed to a database and associated with your profile for other users
to see.

distribution raises questions about how difficult or engaging particular games were, as well as how well they communicated the richer ideas around which they were designed. The Connections game in particular, which aimed to be innovative and was somewhat unusual, might have needed more scaffolding to help iCue users understand the game's potential for learning and for fun.

Are There Relationships among the Activities Users Engage In?

Beyond participants' individual engagement in iCue's activities, we were interested in patterns of activity. For example, did people who had a higher Number of Friends also watch video for longer? Did people seem to make a choice about whether to play games or watch video? Did people who logged in more or who logged in for more than one month perform more activities? Obviously, our data cannot convey causality, so instead we investigated the relationships among our major variables in order to find the best models to describe the predictive relationships among them. In order to determine the major variables, we chose to analyze only those activities engaged in by at least a quarter of iCue's users and combinations of activities that retained at least (a somewhat arbitrary) 15 percent of participants in the sample. Although we tried many models, the ones we describe here are the ones that best fit the data. These analyses do not discuss the effects of age and gender, as they were not predictive in any of our analyses.

In order to gain an insight into what might be bringing users to the site and keeping them there, we analyzed which activities were mostly highly correlated with logins. Seeing that making friends and watching video were the most popular activities, we investigated how well the use of these activities could predict the number of times people logged into iCue. It turns out that knowing about a person's Number of Friends told us more about how much he or she logged in than knowing how much video content that person watched. That is, a typical user would visit the site more if he or she had ten times more friends than if the user had watched ten times as much video.

Figure 10.9a shows that the average Number of Friends a user had for each month logged in increased significantly with each additional month of iCue usage, as one might expect. Users logged in for just one month had a relatively small average Number of Friends (a little over seven),

(a)

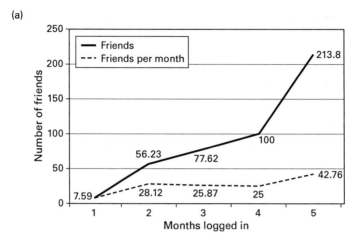

Figure 10.9a

Number of friends by months on iCue. The top line shows the total number of friends as a function of number of months logged in; the bottom line shows new friends acquired by month. Friends show a clear increasing trend over time. Friends per month increases sharply from one month to two and then again from four months to five. The first increase is likely the result of people getting familiar with the site after some time; the latter may be a die-hard group of settlers that stuck together. 1 month, $n = 4324$; 2 months, $n = 699$; 3 months, $n = 269$; 4 months, $n = 80$; 5 months, $n = 36$.

(b)

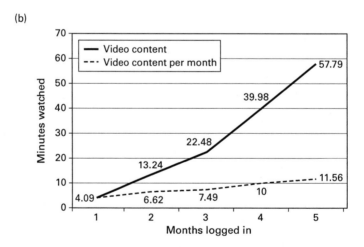

Figure 10.9b

Video content watched by months on iCue. The top line represents the total video watched as a function of months logged in; the bottom line shows the average video watched, accounting for more total time on the site. Both lines show a steady increase over time, meaning that participants not only continued to watch video, but also watched more video per month as they stayed on the site. 1 month, $n = 1258$; 2 months, $n = 596$; 3 months, $n = 238$; 4 months, $n = 76$; 5 months, $n = 3$.

(c)

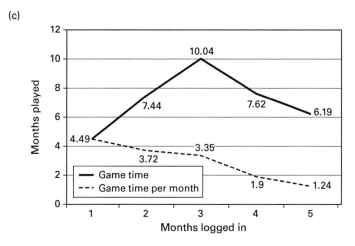

Figure 10.9c

Game time minutes per month on iCue. The top line represents the total time spent playing games as a function of months logged in; the bottom line shows the average game time played for month. Total game time increases for a few months and then decreases, likely indicating that early participants (who had been on the site for some time) were not attracted to the games. The average game time played per month shows a steady decrease by time on the site, reflecting diminishing interest in the games over time. 1 month, $n = 714$; 2 months, $n = 333$; 3 months, $n = 135$; 4 months, $n = 27$; 5 months, $n = 18$.

while each successive month led to more friends, with a large jump for five months (likely representing the pioneers who settled the site as it opened).

As we did with logins, we can see what activities seemed to be associated with having more friends. By far the biggest predictor of Number of Friends is simply the Number of Logins. In other words, people who logged in more were likely to have a high number of friends. As we can't say whether this relationship is causal, it is really just the flip side of the previous analysis—more logins equals more friends. What is notable, however, is that by contrast, users who spent a lot of time playing the games saw a small *decrease* in Number of Friends, all else being equal. However, *submitting* those games played (opening them up to viewing by other people) was associated with a slight *increase* in Number of Friends. We believe this pattern reflects that these games were essentially solitary in their design, pitting the users against themselves, *until* the games were submitted for others to look at on the users' profiles. At this point, the game had become a social "badge of honor" to provoke potentially rich interactions.

We followed the same path in our analysis of the association between Video Content Seconds Watched and Games Time with other patterns of usage. It turned out that users who hung around the site the longest were more likely to watch a higher amount of video. Figure 10.9b shows the steady increase in Video Content Seconds Watched associated with each additional month of site use. Users who continued to three months were watching almost double the video content *per month* when compared to those with only one month of iCue usage on average. Note that they not only watched more video cumulatively but also watched more each month. This statistic indicates that once they got into the site and starting watching video, they wanted to watch more and more—a nod to the quality and value of the video.

The video story stands in sharp contrast to that of the games (figure 10.9c). Although the total Time Playing Games appears to rise slightly initially for the first few months, it falls off after many months on the site. This indicates that people who stayed on the site for a long time were less interested in games. Given the snapshot, this may have represented the early settlers, who came for things other than games. But even looking at that initial increase, when converted into average Time Playing Games per month, there was a steady decrease with each additional month of iCue use—in other words, users who hung around the site for more than a month steadily decreased their monthly game playing. This means that users who stuck around this site for a long time were much more likely to be logging in, making friends, and watching video, but not playing games. In the long run, games didn't seem to capture their interest as much as other iCue activities. If the previous data were a nod to the value and design of the video, these data are further corroboration that the games were not all the team set out to make them.

What Predicts Patterns of Use over Time?

We conducted two more analyses to address questions of usage patterns over time and user longevity. First, we wanted to determine if users were exploring all possible aspects of the site or just sticking with one activity

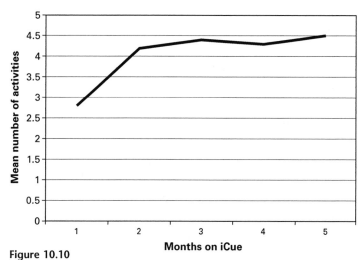

Figure 10.10

Average number of activities per month logged in. Over time, participants tried out more activities, with a big jump in what people tried from months one to two, and then small increases after that.

or just a few. We looked at whether users tried any of the following activities: *logging in, making friends, playing games, watching video,* and *opening CueCards.*

As figure 10.10 shows, the Number of Activities a user engaged in increased significantly when users logged in for more than a month but remained relatively flat thereafter for each additional month. These data suggest that users who continue on the site for more than one month participate in most (four or five) of the available activities, not just one or two, and their exploration outside their core activities is relatively limited.

We also wanted to get further insight into what kept people on the site for more than that initial month. We explored this in several ways, all of which tell basically the same story. We found that the biggest impact on sticking with the site was from Number of Friends, where for every tenfold increase in Number of Friends, people were more than twenty-five times as likely to stay on the site for more than one month. We cannot and do not mean to imply causality, but certainly the people who hung around the site the longest also had a lot of friends. The other activities were also influential, but much less so than Number of Friends. A tenfold increase in Video Content Watched doubled the chances of someone staying on the site, although a tenfold increase in Time Playing Games increased those odds by just 50 percent. Starting on iCue early (defined as August or September, as compared with October or November) also doubled the odds of staying on the site for more than one month (about the same effect as a tenfold increase in video).

These findings suggest that those who were engaged with iCue—by watching content, or making friends, or playing games—were more likely to stick with the site than those who were less engaged. It also suggests that it takes smaller increases in Number of Friends than in amount of Video Content Seconds Watched or Time Playing Games to predict the same increased likelihood of sticking with iCue for more than one month. Additional analyses found that watching more video and making more friends predicted how long someone stayed with the site, but gameplay did not. This finding echoes the earlier finding that Time Playing Games has less potential than other activities for holding participants' long-term interest and attention.

The finding that those who started early were also more likely to stick with the site is interesting. Was there something different about what was happening *on the site* in August and September that made it more compelling? Was there something about *the people* who expressed early interest that made the site more appealing to them? Or, if many of the users were teachers, perhaps those who first logged on in August or September stuck with the site for one more month so that they could use it with their students after school had really started, and those who started in October or November could use it with students right away and therefore didn't need to remain on the site to get full use of it. This may also be explained by the sharp dropoff in iCue staff that happened midway through the period, greatly reducing the daily updates to the site.

What Does All This Mean?

With regard to patterns of use, many people only used iCue a little bit— logging on just a few times within one month and then not continuing. Less than a quarter of those who started using iCue in any month continued using it into a second month. We don't have a benchmark against which to compare these rates—we don't know how this compares to typical rates of attrition for other educational sites, as that data is normally proprietary. ComScore data (Numedon 2011) from Whyville, a web-based educational virtual world built for young teens, indicates that average session time is a little over half an hour for its site, with users visiting the site on average six times per month. It claims that this is several times higher than similar web-based virtual worlds for kids, including Habbo Hotel and Club Penguin.

However, these virtual worlds—and perhaps most other existing educational websites—would provide a poor comparison with iCue anyway. The range of activities possible on iCue makes finding an analogue for comparison difficult. The social network studies mentioned (Gyarmati and Trinh 2010; Benevenuto et al. 2009) do examine behavior across activities. And these studies similarly show that users often focus on a small set of activities that trail off over time. Still, half of all iCue participants logged on at least weekly over the four-and-a-half month period, and there were people who seemed to be regulars—more than five hundred people logged on more than 150 times during this time, for an average of once a day, which is still positive for a new application.

Although our analyses point to different specific relationships among types of activity on iCue, one consistent theme is that—controlling for the Number of Logins—there is a trade-off in how people spent time on the iCue site, *either* playing games, *or* making friends, *or* opening CueCards/watching video content. It is also clear that by the second month of use, most users tried their hand at most, if not all, of the activities. The intention for iCue was to build the audience by providing a variety of activities as entry points and extending residence on the site through additional activities. If users were seeing them as trade-offs, then the site failed. If users were coming to the site for a single activity that they really liked, though, they seemed to stick around longer and were more likely to try all the activities.

Regardless of how the site was being used, it wasn't being used by many people. Perhaps that wasn't such a bad thing. In 2003, usability expert Jakob Nielsen wrote compellingly that having a small but dedicated audience can be quite powerful: "Small sites speak directly to the specific needs and interests of a committed user community, and thus have much higher value per page view. . . . Diversity is power on the Web. Big sites may be bigger, but smaller sites will keep scoring higher for specialized topics, both in terms of their connections with users and in terms of each visit's commercial value." But NBC News was not going to be comfortable serving a niche audience with iCue. Not everyone who surfs the Web would need a site such as this, but teachers and history buffs of all ages could find a home in iCue's forums. Only a small percentage (12–25 percent) of those who started using iCue in any month continued using it into a second month. This number is not particularly atypical in the new media frontier; riding long tails in this way is central to such online megaluminaries as social microblogging site Twitter and the massively multiplayer online game World of Warcraft. Recent data suggest that only about 19 percent of all Twitter users are actually using their accounts at all (Moore 2010), but Twitter is potentially a poor comparison, as it is a site that exists solely for the purpose of social networking. World of Warcraft may be a (slightly) better analogue to iCue, as it allows users to network through a series of activities, although it is a qualitatively different, robust 3D game universe. World of Warcraft's makers, Activision Blizzard, recently released the data showing that only about 30 percent of players who try the free trial account go on to take their characters past level 10 (out of 85) (Torres 2010)—not too far from iCue's number.

What may have been more of a concern than the small audience was the decline in users and logins over time. If the content seemed too static to users, or was difficult or confusing to interact with, they likely would have spent their time on the Web somewhere else. Likewise, if adult teachers (or learners) saw the site as pitched to them in commercials on MSNBC or direct marketing in schools, only to find messaging aimed at teenagers, they might have been disinclined to investigate the site.

Ultimately, iCue was too expensive to create and inadequately incubated to survive, meaning that the committed crowd of regulars would be ousted from its online home. The reach for the education market sealed the fate of iCue's innovations, and the site was ultimately closed down.

11　What Next?

iCue: RIP 2005–2011

Don't look for iCue on NBC News website; you won't find it. On February 1, 2011, the site was taken down and users were migrated to a free trial of the NBC Learn platform, the ultimate evolution of the Archives on Demand product and home to NBC's education initiatives, staffed mostly by the drivers of iCue.

For a time, NBC News continued to trickle resources into iCue to keep it somewhat fresh, but they could not justify the continued cost of maintenance for this scarcely used product. But Archives on Demand had taken off. Using the lessons learned from iCue, as well as its technology, production methods, and video archives, the product line grew. Without the overhead of creating games and essay questions or maintaining a social network, the curators of Archives on Demand could focus on populating the media archive for a broad range of subjects. Gone are the participatory elements, the games, and anything targeting students directly—iCue's principal legacy is solely the CueCard, which has migrated to the streaming archival product, as well as many other projects across NBC News. Perhaps more important to the success of this product is that it is not broadly marketed to students and teachers, homes and schools, but squarely to schools, which are more easily enticed by a vast, teacher-facing video archive with connections to many different subject areas.

It isn't hard to understand why iCue disappeared. It wasn't being used. NBC News built it, only a small number of teachers showed up, and the students never came. Jones has chalked up some of this to marketing and the inability to market to the student audience that he and his colleagues wanted to reach. He conceded that the study-aid market was a bust and that the only way the team was going to get students to use the system themselves was to "require it" through school. And teacher adoption was extremely difficult. Most teachers who saw the resource were enthusiastic but without purchasing power. An even greater body of teachers still operated under a top-down model of curated information delivery and weren't comfortable with opening up that resource directly to the students to explore and discover on their own. Jones says:

Why is there some reluctance to let it open up and to let students play with it? And you say, today they start that journey of self-discovery. You're taking a raw piece of information and instead of saying it's curated—or it's an opinion that the teacher would give—look at the raw elements and look at the story and how it's built, and you make an assessment and think about what it means. So that's probably the biggest surprise I've seen. When you look at the usage of raw [information] it's not being pushed down to the students, and we probably have to do a better job of messaging that.

Further, the experience of trying to make iCue work brought about the realization that NBC News didn't have the internal capacity for creating the social networking and gaming aspects that the iCue experience hinged on.

Don't look for Adam Jones at NBC News, either. He too has gone, having migrated back to his home in England to be the CFO of another media company.

Despite the conspicuous absence of iCue and Jones himself from the NBC News organization, the mission of NBC News to contribute significantly to education lives on. That this continued mission within the organization has lived beyond the original champion and product is a noteworthy measure of institutional change. Although the manifestation of this change bears only a passing resemblance to the initial vision that Chisholm, Williams, Jones, and we ourselves had several years ago, it lives on nonetheless.

Success behind the Paywall

The shift in products and strategy demanded a change in how the product was supported. Most of the content is now behind a "paywall" that requires a subscription—either institutional or individual. This model follows the one that many other media companies are using, from newspapers to television. Among NBC Learn's institutional customers is one 800-pound gorilla. The University of Phoenix partnership, which began during the production of the Facebook game, successfully bridged the gap from iCue to NBC Learn. It remains a substantial contributor to the NBC Learn effort. The University of Phoenix has licensed access to all of the Archives on Demand for use in its courses and has partnered with NBC News on additional educational ventures. Because it is the largest private university in the country, this relationship has resulted in a reasonable amount of revenue for NBC Learn. It has also brought some desirable credibility for the University of Phoenix by association, theoretically reducing some of the stigma it has developed from being pulled into court over its business practices regularly since 2000. It remains to be seen whether the University of Phoenix will get this part of its house in order and have a long-term impact on the way eLearning and distance learning are conducted, but it is undeniable that its presence in higher education has forced some traditional universities and colleges into online and blended learning. In this respect alone, as another for-profit company, NBC News is sensible to partner with a leader in online education.

NBC Learn has also managed to include another online learning behemoth, Blackboard, in its arsenal of significant corporate clients. Blackboard is the largest provider of online course-management systems, servicing well over 10,000 institutions nationwide. Schools that use Blackboard are also able to purchase site licenses and integrate NBC Learn's content. These two clients alone would provide a significant backbone to any online learning initiative.

It is not hard to see why the Archives on Demand work in these contexts, whereas iCue would not. iCue was an open-ended, student-centered product with perhaps too great a diversity in activities. It would be hard for a teacher or professor to separate out sections of the experience and embed them in his or her own materials, for instance. By contrast, the Archives on Demand are bite-sized nuggets designed exclusively for embedding in other contexts. In fact, they do little on their own. But teachers and professors are always looking for good resources to use in their own courses, and the Archives on Demand make it easy and legal to embed these tagged and course-correlated resources. The flippable CueCard media player allows some additional interactivity through tagging and sharing, which makes it just a little more than a standard media asset as well.

This ease of use has enabled the NBC Learn team to sell additional subscriptions at the secondary and postsecondary levels directly. Through a sales force numbering around twenty-five, it has managed to sell subscriptions to K–12 schools and universities. What is currently a nationwide sales effort may be pared back at some point to focus on markets with higher success rates. In an interview he gave as he was departing NBC News, Jones said that he sees future efforts focusing on "parts of the country [where] we've got clear opportunities—Texas, Florida, the northeast corridor. [We can] focus there and build a base there, rather than diluting our marketing and PR efforts across the country, just focus on certain markets and leverage the local affiliates to help out." Unable to find a suitable distribution partner, Jones grew his own with the help of some resources he had all along.

Foundation Relations

Jones has also managed to develop a unique business model in order to sustain NBC Learn. He estimates that nearly 40 percent of the NBC Learn revenue came from the University of Phoenix, with another 20–25 percent coming from subscription deals. The remaining portion came from foundations (corporate and private) to do "special projects." The first of these projects arose through a meeting that Chisholm arranged with several large foundations. At first the mission of the for-profit NBC News didn't seem to mesh with that of the foundations, but Jones tries to emphasize the positive:

I went out with Alex [Chisholm] to the foundation meeting last summer and we sat around for most of the day that I was presenting. We talked about what we planned. Obviously we're the big, bad for-profit. I said, you know, there are a couple of fundamentals. We've invested in [education on] a scale that probably very few other media programs would do on something like this. But we're in the businesses of making and distributing content. So the fact that NBC Learn and iCue [are] built on a caching structure, eighty thousand servers globally . . . when you think about that investment, that is shared by the whole of NBC Universal, we're able to do things at a scale and a pace that's really hard to match.

Still, he didn't seem to get much traction, so he decided to push a little harder:

And at the end of that day, when all the thought leaders sat around the table and said, what does everyone think? How effective has today's presentation been? And

I put my hand up and said, "You know, do I have permission to speak freely?" They said, "Yes," and I said, "You know, I will leave this meeting and I will think that it has been a large waste of time because all you ever do is talk about stuff. Or you don't do it at a scale that really makes a difference. . . . The textbook publishers wouldn't work with me, some of the early foundations wouldn't work with me, I had internal resistance from the organization [NBC News] and [I feel] like I'm doing this journey alone . . . and I keep going forward. But someone, for God's sake, step up and do something. You know, you have strategic needs. I mean, let's find a way. Let's do something."

And after that a guy came up to me and said, "Let's do something." So the Kellogg Foundation has now funded a series called "Finishing the Dream." If you go onto iCue right now, there's a series called "Finishing the Dream" which then charts the civil rights movement and you go back to some really iconic stuff.

Though "Finishing the Dream" began its life in iCue, it got moved to the outer layer of NBC Learn, where it can be found in a section of "original video" content produced for the NBC Learn site.

The next foundation to step in was the NSF:

We met with the National Science Foundation last summer [2009] and they saw some of the content and said "You guys are doing really, really great educational content. One of the things that we are very concerned about is that there are amazing things happening in the world of science on a daily basis. You know, blind people can see, cars run on water, but you know, outside of the science community no one cares and it's a real problem. Science is no longer seen as an obvious career choice and we're seeing that graduation rates are going down. . . . Could you come up with an idea of doing something cool with science?"

So our team had gone away and we sat down and we brainstormed and said, "OK, we're going to come up with a concept called the Science of the Winter Olympics." And we built it, taking conservation of angular momentum, Newton's first three laws of motion, you know, friction, and built videos using historical Olympics, which is based on the relationship with the U.S. Olympic Committee. Leveraging our production capabilities and NBC Sports and getting exclusive access to the athletes and then interviewing NSF funded scientists to help them explain the science behind it and wrapping it all up into these short-form videos. We produced this really, really high-class, I mean, the highest quality production. It's probably the first example I've ever seen where we actually produce content for the Web. . . . It was a special collection on iCue, [and] it got repurposed for the broadcast, so over 175 of our 200 affiliates took the contents and played it on the air during the Olympics.

This was indeed an unusual event: content produced for the Web migrated to the broadcast news. The Science of the Olympics was a success both in terms of generating traffic to NBC Learn and for meeting the NSF's goals. At the annual meeting of the National Association of Science Teachers later that year, NBC Learn was present to show its wares, and the NSF was also there. The NSF team came over to the NBC Learn team to tell them that half of its visitors came to thank it for the recent Science of the Olympics. That kind of gratitude yielded a similar collaboration among NBC Learn, the NSF, and the National Football League (NFL) to create the Science of the NFL, launched on NBC Learn in the fall of 2010. Again, the originally produced video appears on a special site outside the NBC Learn paywall, providing a service but also driving traffic to the site. The combination of the Winter Olympics and NFL science efforts resulted in a Sports Emmy awarded to NBC Learn in 2011.

Channeling Frustration

Despite the success of these partnerships, subscriptions, and collaborations, the NBC Learn initiative was quite costly, and has a long way to go to recoup costs. Says Jones,

Probably net investment today in iCue, net loss, is probably $25 million. That's a lot of—so I have lost a lot of money, and I have continued to have Jeff Zucker and others be critical. And I have said, "Think about what has been done. That is not a loss. That is an investment in 10,000 plus pieces." So I have really said in terms of breaking the back of digitizing the archives, I have made a very, very significant start. And the organizations now are starting to wake up to that. So for me, had the organization thought and planned and invested in the archives [as] they should have done, you know, five years before I got here, that investment would have been a fraction of what it ended up having to be because I had to take it all on and I took it on for the organization in perpetuity rather than just clearing it for the U.S. education market only. I made the decision to do it for everything, in perpetuity, which was the right decision, but just a bigger investment. And at the end of the day $25 million isn't huge given how big [the organization] is. It's doable.

Jones offered sound reasons for his departure—running to new opportunities as the CFO of a large British media company and a return to his homeland and family. But the frustration with both the organization and the educational landscape still comes through loud and clear. He is critical of the organization's hostile environment for innovation:

This is an old media company that is not engineered around innovation. And that's the fundamental problem that it faces. Innovation is key to growth. And the cost cutting, which is what you've seen pervasively, obviously is death by a thousand cuts. Even the fact that we started the iCue investments and the creation of the technology back in 2006, had I waited until even [2008], it just would never have happened. So there was that window and I had a sense of it and I could manage it and I was in a position to control it.

And he sees an equally hostile environment for innovation in the world of K–12 schools: "The education market simply isn't structured to support innovation in learning and that simply has to change. We can have that conversation and obviously we have experience and we're at the table to talk about it."

In a July 2011 interview with the *Wall Street Journal*, Bill Gates echoes these feelings of frustration intervening in schools. He is quoted as saying, "It's hard to improve public education—that's clear. As Warren Buffett would say, if you're picking stocks, you wouldn't pick this one." Despite these challenges, Jones, like Gates, remains passionate about education. The frustration he found endemic in both systems made him seek new solutions: "I think the education is incredibly important. In hindsight, it was far more difficult than I ever thought it would be and that frustration is one of the reasons that kept driving me, trying to make a difference. It's a classic old school media company that just doesn't incubate startups like it should and that [also] makes it very, very difficult."

Although he didn't know it at the time, Jones was to plan one last hurrah at NBC News. He was frustrated with both the inability to change the organization and the inability to make the slightest impact on education. The solution was to get NBC News behind a high-profile event focused on education, ultimately called Education Nation. Jones had been planning an event for some time and seized upon yet another high-profile election to enact his plan:

Having made the suggestion and planted the seed in the NBC News management's mind and then with the help of Lisa Gersh [president of strategic initiatives] up to the executive office at the chairman's level with Jeff Zucker to say, "We can make a powerful statement about education. It's an issue that is pretty crucial to America's competitive future, and it's not really been addressed in the mainstream media. We at NBC have an opportunity to really sort of take control and own this space and obviously we ourselves are committed to education through NBC Learn so it can come together and although I wouldn't want to present Education Nation as purely a platform to promote NBC Learn, but since we have skin in the game and we're heavily invested in the education market, we think we have a very valid play."

The challenge, yet again, was funding. Once again, the University of Phoenix came on board in a big way, as did a number of corporations such as Raytheon and foundations such as the Bill and Melinda Gates Foundation. Through our connection with Jones, Klopfer finagled his way into the event through a back door, covering the event as a journalist for this book.

Education Nation

NBC News billed the event as follows:

Education Nation is a nationally broadcast, in-depth conversation about improving education in America. During an interactive summit on Rockefeller Plaza, parents, teachers, and students will come together with leaders in politics, business, and technology to discuss the challenges and opportunities in education today. In addition, NBC News will turn Rockefeller Plaza into a "Learning Plaza," a series of five galleries, open to the public, which will allow visitors to explore America's educational "ecosystem." During the entire week, NBC News will highlight education stories as well as broadcast live from the Plaza.

And NBC defined the mission of the event thus: "Education Nation seeks to engage the public, through thoughtful dialogue, in pursuit of the shared goal of providing every American with an opportunity to pursue the best education in the world." (2010, http://educationnation.com). NBC went on to describe the problems in education relating to graduation rates, global competitiveness, and workforce development. And finally, it made the following commitment:

We believe that providing quality news and information to the public—the hallmark of journalistic excellence—will help Americans make decisions about how best to improve our education system. NBC News is committed to gathering policymakers and thought-leaders annually for an informed, enlightened discussion of the challenges, potential solutions and innovations spanning the education landscape. This discussion will be highlighted for a national audience across all NBC News platforms. We will continue our coverage to hold our leaders and communities accountable for improving outcomes in the near and long terms. NBC News will follow this story until this mission is fulfilled.

Although it may be easy to dismiss the event as a publicity gimmick to get the audience to focus on its brand of news about an issue that is clearly near and dear to the public, the scale of the commitment to this event and subsequent follow-up indicates that the level of involvement is much deeper than that. It seems to be an organizational commitment to changing education, a commitment that is hard to imagine having occurred four or five years earlier, before the rise of NBC Learn out of iCue and its progeny.

The Social Media Event

The event officially started with the Teacher Town Hall hosted by Brian Williams on a Sunday afternoon in September 2010. But because this was a twenty-first-century event, its real start was several weeks earlier, online. The Education Nation Facebook page went online and was quickly populated with lively discussions by teachers, parents, and professionals interested in education. A theme quickly emerged on the site. Where are the teachers? Though the event did kick off with the Teacher Town Hall on Sunday, the "real" event was clearly the following two days. Those panels were populated with foundation representatives, corporate CEOs, a few university faculty members, and several public personalities. Teachers were largely absent and immediately felt left out of the conversation.

Further, teachers perceived a town hall on a Sunday afternoon in September to be in a television ghetto. Between postseason baseball and the football season going into high gear, those who weren't in church wouldn't likely be tuning into MSNBC for Teacher Town Hall coverage at that time. This situation created a legitimate perception that a large corporate entity outside education intended to swoop in and "solve" all of education's problems. Those in the trenches deeply resented this perspective. And, as is the case in most social media discussions online, the comments fired at NBC weren't subtle. For instance:

I don't see a single person listed in this extravaganza who is not a publicist for the corporatizing, centralized, corporate-philanthropy-driven, anti-democratic version of "reform" being foisted on our cities by people who claim to care more about our kids than our citizens do. If these ideas are so brilliant, let's hear how they stand up to criticism. Why is the national press so complacent on this subject? Why are they so unconcerned about the effects of these policies on their own constituents? I hope they're tougher on banking reform.

and:

The billionaires, think-tankers, and hedge-funders are the ones who should be marginalized as "other voices." Students, parents and teachers are the heart of our schools and should be the dominant voices in this discussion. NBC, this is an assault against families and schools, not to mention a PR fiasco.

Steve Capus, president of NBC News, was quoted in a response on the Facebook wall: "You can't have a conversation about education, let alone a two-day summit and week of broadcasting around these issues, without the participation of teachers, parents, and students." But that wasn't enough for many people, with one person going so far as to say that he or she didn't understand why "rank-and-file K–12 teachers and parents aren't at least half of the conveners of the core summit."

Bloggers also pointed to the presence of the University of Phoenix among both the sponsors and the speakers, implying that it had paid for a place at the table. The comments kept flying so fast and furiously that NBC News ultimately moved the Facebook page to a moderated status, which perturbed the audience enough to create a counter Facebook page called "MisEducation Nation," which attracted a few hundred people.

The critiques from Facebook (and a similar Twitter discussion on the #EducationNation tag) aside, the event that NBC News put together was certainly unique in the scale and makeup of the audience. It seemed apparent that NBC News listened to the feedback and tried to bring teachers into most of the panels and get them into the audience as well. The presence of so many foundations, corporations, public personalities, media companies, and educational approaches put the event in a class of its own. With the media clout of NBC News to bring the proceedings to the world, it was clear that the event would make some kind of mark.

The Road to Change

The event officially opened with the Teacher Town Hall. *NBC Nightly News* anchor Brian Williams took the stage under a tent in Rockefeller Plaza where the skating rink usually is. Prominent in the background was the plaza's golden statue of Prometheus (figure 11.1).

Although the event wasn't as large in spatial scale as the big Las Vegas launch party for iCue, it shared some of the grandeur and polish of that event—the intent to put one's best foot forward. This time, the NBC News talent was there in person. This time, though, they were promoting not a product, but an idea.

Figure 11.1
Inside the tent at the Teacher Town Hall.

Williams opened the event with a few candid remarks. First, he noted that the tent that we were all in (there were a few hundred people in attendance) was not the one that was originally intended. The original plans called for a custom inflatable dome with the Education Nation logo. That dome had worked perfectly until workers actually tried to inflate it the night before, when it became clear that it wasn't going to work.

Second, Williams cited great influential teachers in his own life, but somewhat apologetically acknowledged that although our goal was to get more kids into and graduating from college, he himself had not actually graduated from college and was "lucky enough to find a profession where that wasn't a barrier." To those in the audience, this seemed like another indication of the lack of grounding in education on the part of the NBC News group.

Despite this acknowledgment, Williams navigated the Teacher Town Hall with aplomb. There were several featured teachers—teachers of the year, teachers from tough schools who had done wonderful things, and teachers who had learned from experiences around the world. But the comments of the teachers in the town hall audience didn't reflect those themes much; those in the audience just wanted to voice their opinions. Predictable controversies arose—charter schools versus district schools, teachers' unions, merit pay, tenure, administrators, and outside intrusions from people (or institutions) who don't really understand what is going on inside schools. Many of these issues reflected what made implementing iCue in schools difficult. It would be hard to say that this conversation advanced much during this time, or that solutions were found, but given the diverse audience, it did perhaps get everyone (including anyone viewing at home) on the same page about what the big issues are. In the process, this unproductive debate gave some ammunition to outsiders frustrated by the lack of change from the inside.

The Teacher Town Hall was followed up later that night with a screening of Davis Guggenheim's movie *Waiting for Superman*. *Waiting for Superman* shone a national spotlight on some of the issues facing public schools, many of which were voiced during the afternoon session by the teachers themselves. Guggenheim did, in the opinion of many, identify a clear solution to the problem—charter schools. The movie champions leaders in the charter school movement such as Geoffrey Canada, successful schools such as the Knowledge Is Power Program (KIPP) charters, and reformers who take on the unions, such as Michelle Rhee. It vilifies unions as the great roadblock for all things wonderful in schools, the keepers of tenure and saviors of bad teachers everywhere. The movie was in turn followed by a discussion with many of the "stars" of the movie, including Rhee and the president of the American Federation of Teachers, Randi Weingarten. The familiar issues of tenure, unions, and charters appeared again. Though there were clearly points of contention, in this case it appeared that there were at times places for agreement.

Although the details of this premiere may seem like a diversion, the movie takes a strong stand—a stand that is supported increasingly by Democrats and Republicans alike: there should be more charter schools, more freedom, and less interference from the unions. Despite support from both sides, this is still a controversial position, as there are ample data to call into question how "successful" some of these solutions are. Questions are raised by many about the general applicability of the lessons from of KIPP schools, the lasting change available through charters, and the kind of knowledge gained at these schools. Though NBC News may have initially intended merely to bring the issues to light, the spotlight on this movie and its message indicated not only that these issues were going to be brought to light, but also that people would take a stand.

When the event opened on Monday morning, Tom Brokaw took the stage. The rain started audibly to pour upon the white vinyl (and possibly hastily constructed) roof. A series of unlikely events—including President Obama being remotely interviewed by Matt Lauer; New York City's mayor, Michael Bloomberg, being forced to broadcast a statement from a back studio; and Facebook founder Mark Zuckerberg (who had just donated $100 million to the Newark city schools) being rushed off the stage as the roof indicated it might collapse—brought a sense of chaos to the event.

As the pages in the building smiled and tried to tell the participants where to go, people behind the scenes tried to find places to send everyone. Once again, NBC's education initiative would be stuffed into any available studio. This resulted in some unlikely, and possibly ironic, scenarios, including Tom Brokaw's interview of Secretary of Education Arne Duncan in *Saturday Night Live*'s storied Studio 8H (figure 11.2).

Figure 11.2
Live, from Studio 8H, Tom Brokaw and Arne Duncan.

Throughout that session and the rest of the day, every panel rehashed the same themes:

• Everyone needs a quality teacher in the classroom.

• We know what works. There are examples of successful strategies that should be replicated.

• It is about the kids, not the teachers. Don't let union squabbles get in the way.

• Hiring and firing. We need to get rid of the worst teachers and find incentives to hire the best.

• Everyone needs to be involved. This includes parents, teachers, administrators, students, and leaders.

• Teachers need accountability that doesn't need to be narrow. Teachers should be accountable for results, but not necessarily test results.

• School needs to prepare students for the modern workplace. The twentieth-century school, designed for the industrial era, is no longer adequate.

• We can serve the neediest. We now know they can perform well academically, when given the chance.

It isn't clear that we really know "what works," but there were some clear examples of things working throughout the summit.

Emerging from Education Nation

By most measures, Education Nation was a success. Perhaps the most important unit of measure in the old media business is TV households, and Jones related that the impact of the event was quite broad—more than 50 million TV households were reached. He also acknowledged that there was still room for improvement. The messaging to the sponsors needed work. Some sponsors incorrectly believed that they would get commercial airtime as a result of their sponsorship, and it will take some work to get those sponsors back. Still, the University of Phoenix was slated to come back in 2011 with a "significant" sponsorship, including a road show that would take the message around the country, not just to Rockefeller Plaza. That roadshow has since started.

Jones also talked about the shortcomings in messaging not only to the sponsors, but to the educators who had expressed their concerns on Facebook and elsewhere around the Internet: "There was significant backlash from the teacher population to say, "Why didn't you invite Diane Ravitch?" . . . We made very concerted efforts to have a balanced conversation and get lots of people in, including Diane as just one example. . . . So it had its challenge in terms of messaging. We could have done a better job, but we had a very balanced conversation."

A Two-Pronged Attack

So why did NBC News put on such a huge production? The expense and complexity make it seem an unlikely event for a news organization to pursue. At first glance, it didn't seem to support initiatives such as iCue directly at all. There are many possible answers to this question.

On the surface, the answer that Education Nation delivered was that education is a critical issue to the nation's future—and one that gets lost in media coverage. Shining a spotlight on it in a fairly significant way was important for raising public awareness about this issue, and this is the job of the media. Critics suggest that the event was not journalistic coverage of the topic but merely a vehicle for billionaire philanthropists to advance their educational-change agenda. We assert that those critics might have it backward. Instead, perhaps the billionaire philanthropists were being used as a lever to effect change. From where we sit, the impetus for the event was Jones's frustration (and that of others on the NBC Learn team) over not being able to effect even the slightest change in the public schools. The team had an innovation that seemed in all ways like something that teachers, schools, and students should embrace. Instead, it met many forms of resistance—resistance from schools in the way they purchase educational products, resistance from textbook publishers in the way they value digital media, resistance from teachers to put digital media in the hands of their students, and resistance from consumers to paying for web-delivered products. This resistance planted in the organization a desire to change the system, to pave the road not just for future products but for future innovations that the NBC Learn team believed can and should take place in schools.

Building the product, making it available, and showing all of the AP teachers how great it was didn't lead to adoption or change. Clearly, the system needed changing, so that path to change needed to come not only from innovative products but also from political and social pressure for change. Education Nation was the way to do this by raising national attention to issues faced in schools and by bringing to the table people who were already at work trying to effect change. Even if not all interests were aligned, just kicking the hornet's nest was a place to start.

The final answer is that Jones and those he left behind firmly believe that education is the future of their business. Jones went so far as to say, "I think the mandate of NBC News over time will change. . . . I would think if we chart this course and continue that ultimately the education business will make more money than the broadcast side will. And I think ultimately that [the education group will] sustain the newsgathering." So how could that happen? Jones gave his vision for how things could play out in the next couple of years:

I'm going to guess [that NBC Learn is] probably a $10 million–plus subscription business, probably has won a number of educational software awards and is recognized as an industry leader in supplementary material. . . . Within five years, I would say it will be the number one educational video subscription service out there. . . . I would see usage of the product outside the U.S. as well.

Realizing this vision would make NBC Learn a significant product in the portfolio of NBC News and would be a necessary, but perhaps not sufficient, effort to sustain the organization, given recent media trends. Americans across all age groups are watching less television and getting much of their information (including news) from the Internet. Their phones are replacing their televisions.[5] And this news doesn't come from just one source, either. Thanks to Americans' use of online tools such as RSS Aggregators, and aggregation sites as diverse as Google News and the Huffington Post, it will be harder for a brand such as NBC News to get the loyalty it might have been given in the days before the Internet, and certainly before widespread broadband.

With Jones's departure, and without a replacement for him, the mission of innovation through education is now being carried on by iCue producers Gage, Miano, and Nissen, and by Levin (now working with both the technology and the marketing) and others—as they continue to pursue education as a means of stabilizing journalism. No longer is today's news tomorrow's birdcage liner. It is instead truly history's first draft. It is of note that they now face an education market that has changed somewhat in the last few years—slow, significant, and positive change. The Common Core Standards are emerging, which will align (at least partially) the disparate standards that each state has established for itself, making the process of introducing a project nationwide a bit easier and less costly. New

---

5. In 2010, the Pew Research Center announced data indicating that 42 percent of Americans think TV is a luxury as opposed to a necessity, down 10 percent from 2006. In the eighteen- to twenty-nine-year-old demographic, that figure is 29 percent. In a different study, Pew researchers reported that Americans are still spending roughly the same amount of time online as they were in 2006 across all age groups, but that the venue may be changing. Mobile phones have expanded their reach as wireless Internet devices, with 28 percent of teens and 35 percent of adults using their phones to access content online. Figures for teens getting news online remain roughly constant (62 percent in 2010) since 2000, with spikes in election years such as 2004 and 2006. The percentage of adults getting their news online has also been constant since 2002 (71 percent in 2010), with 68 percent saying they go online specifically for political news (Pew 2010).

Media Literacies and similar sets of twenty-first-century skills are being taken seriously and are even being considered as parts of standardized exams such as the National Assessment of Educational Progress. And many teachers are beginning to better understand social networks; some are thinking about how to extend them to their students. None of these developments, or even the sum of these, makes the education market innovation friendly, but they do suggest that as this team moves forward and introduces (or reintroduces) innovations, it may have an easier time.

12 What If?

Mark Miano, producer of the iCue government course:

The original concept of iCue with friending, the social-networking piece of it, was of really big interest to me—the idea of it becoming a collaborative learning environment. . . . Those big ideas about iCue were what really attracted me to the project.

I think the verdict on iCue is still out there. Right now we never unlocked that friending feature in a way where you really felt connected to people. It's very hard to find friends, and when you make a friend it's very hard to communicate with those friends [because of COPPA regulations]. And so I just felt like it never really got unlocked in the way that it could still be, and may still be. So I hope it does because I think that's a valuable tool.

Soraya Gage, producer of the iCue US History course:

I'd like to get gaming back in. To make really compelling games is a huge investment. We tried to do them ourselves, and the games we created for iCue were never used [by iCue users]. The results were poor. But I would like gaming; I'd like more community. The forum was the most popular part of iCue.

Nicola Soares, former vice president of marketing:

We just didn't have the money. We weren't in a position to fund it. To be able to generate and create [content] and do everything it takes is very expensive. The market's definitely ready for it, and students and teachers are doing all sorts of really interesting things.

What Wasn't

In the final analysis, iCue may have tried to be too many things for too many people. It's unclear which direction might have been the "right" one, although it is tempting to use the relative success of the online streaming product to say that those features compose the "right" model. By trying to please teens and teachers, and by offering an overwhelming range of options right from the start, iCue may have let users get lost. But then again, those users were proportionately no less "lost" than on other popular successes such as Twitter and World of Warcraft, despite a sharp dropoff in fresh content. What is clear is that iCue did not cause a revolution. It did not forever change learning, making it self-directed or communal. The innovation of iCue did not diffuse. It is enlightening to compare the unsuccessful (in terms of market penetration) iCue product with the Archives on Demand that continue to survive and thrive along the metrics for diffusion established by Rogers (2003), introduced in chapter 8.

Relative advantage   iCue may be compared to traditional AP test-prep books and software. For students, iCue may have been more fun and engaging than those alternative methods, but if their goal was simply to do well on the existing AP exam, the other methods were more efficient, cheaper, and proven. For teachers, iCue could likely be compared to alternative homework assignments. From this perspective, iCue didn't connect students and teachers or provide easy ways for teachers to manage classes and assignments. It also didn't allow them to customize or pick and choose activities. The Archives on Demand, by contrast, might be comparable to other video sources online. The Archives on Demand allow for a curated experience with tagged video, related notes, and video edited for the classroom—a clear advantage over searching for resources on the Web.

Compatibility   iCue's strength—and ultimately, one of its big weaknesses—was its compatibility with contemporary student media practices and its corresponding incompatibility with school practices. For students, iCue could have provided ways of engaging with school learning that were aligned well with the online practices in which they participated regularly outside school. In practice, the way that those activities were manifested within the site was a poor reflection of students' actual practices, making the experience less compatible in practice than it was by design. From a teacher's perspective, iCue was a radical departure from the assignments that most teachers give in their AP classes. The use of media, the games, and the open-endedness were decidedly incompatible with what most teachers *did*, though for a small portion of teachers the activities were compatible with what they *wanted* to do. The Archives on Demand stand in sharp contrast. They allow for teacher-directed models that are still the most common way of teaching and learning. Teachers can simply integrate the Archives on Demand directly into their lectures in a modular fashion.

Complexity The early reviews of iCue commended it for its breadth of activities but offered the critique that it was hard to know where to go and what to do. The richest of the activities (some of the games) had the added complexity of user interfaces that weren't designed by game/user experience experts, obfuscating much of the learning and fun. iCue was also designed as a stand-alone portal, making it complex to think about how resources and activities from within iCue could be used elsewhere. The Archives on Demand use the simple interface of the CueCard to display video that can be embedded elsewhere and used offline. The CueCard is one of the simpler and more elegant video players out there, and the Archives on Demand are primarily about that interface.

Trialability iCue scores well on trialability. Students and teachers could both try it out at no cost. The question was what could be gained by using iCue on a relatively short-term, limited basis. It was really designed to be used for an entire course, and many of the gains would come only from more regular use. The Archives on Demand, though a paid product, do offer a free trial to teachers. The Science of the Winter Olympics, the Science of the NFL, and other similarly sponsored components are also free to everyone, providing another opportunity to sample the product without paying. It is also easy to see how using just a small number of assets from the Archives on Demand could have immediate value.

Observability Through its integrated social networks, iCue had the potential to offer observability. Friends could see one another's work and share with one another. However, the social network was so muted that these sharing features were rarely used (e.g., posting in the forums and submitting games for review rarely occurred). There was also no visibility outside iCue. One couldn't post anything in a publicly visible way, or to other social networks. The Archives on Demand allow sharing of CueCards with colleagues, but perhaps most of the observability comes from teachers showing their work to others.

The evidence here clearly points to the Archives on Demand being an innovation that was poised to be diffused, whereas iCue was not. It should be noted, however, that success in market penetration isn't the same as success in school reform or other learning revolutions. Although the iCue

product died, the revolutionary ideas continue on within NBC Learn—
NBC Learn is creating new pathways to innovation. The seeds of social
networking and gaming for learning planted by Chisholm and the Education Arcade remain with the team that persists, as demonstrated by the
quotations that begin this chapter. It is tempting to pile on the perceived
failure of iCue and ask any number of "what if" questions. What if the site
had been more modest in its ambitions early on, hewing closer to the
original vision that Chisholm initially laid out? What if NBC News was
convinced at the highest levels from the beginning that digitizing the
archives would be a valuable practice for the entire organization, freeing
the iCue unit from bearing the full cost and risk of the process? What if
NBC News had an internal culture devoted to incubation, allowing iCue
to iterate its way to real innovation without needing to generate revenue
immediately? There are many "what if" questions that could be considered, and future ventures at NBC News and elsewhere may help shed some
light on those questions. Ultimately, though, we can only speculate about
the particular case of iCue. We feel it is important to imagine where the
participatory and potentially innovative elements of iCue could have gone
based on contemporary theory and practice.

Although there are many sources of resistance to change within the
institution of education, high among those are the current (often high-
stakes) standardized tests. Most of these tests are capable of only fairly
superficial assessments of understanding, and most stick to an easy-to-test
set of facts and figures. The limitations of these instruments, and the standards from which they are derived, are increasingly being challenged. More
twenty-first-century skills (such as those produced by the Partnership for
21st Century Skills) are now creeping into the standards and are being used
in assessments by researchers. They are even being adopted in standardized
assessments such as the National Assessment of Educational Progress
(NAEP) and ultimately finding their way into schools. This change is exem-
plified by the recent overhaul of much of the AP curriculum and tests,
including AP History (Drew 2011), moving well beyond recall of names,
dates, and places to focus on deeper understandings of historical context
and consequences. It may now be a question of *when* we will see schools
using more student-centric activities and curricula in schools, not *if* we
will see such change.

Early in its development, iCue was to provide users with online studios
to remix NBC footage and upload user-generated content, as well as oppor-

tunities for mentorship in journalism through contact with iCue producers as modeled in TEA's journalism competition. But in the end, limited resources and concerns from NBC's Standards and Practices unit made such initiatives all but impossible. "What if a kid creates video that shows Martin Luther King palling around with Hitler or something? Or creates racist or otherwise offensive content with the NBC Peacock on it?" producers and executives would say. It was difficult to get them to recognize the value of cocreating media with members of their new audience, mentoring the students and sharing NBC's own best practices. They could not rely on the potential of a community to grow from the bottom up and to police itself. These programs could have brought attention to iCue from young people and stirred interest among adults who might have fit into iCue's "long tail" of committed users.

Ito and colleagues (2009, 17) indicate that teenage life online is focused on three "genres" of participation: "hanging out, messing around, and geeking out." Each genre reflects a differing level of investment in new media activities. The teens in their studies could move fluidly among varying levels of interaction, but their behaviors frequently hung together in these genres. "Hanging out" encompasses friend-driven behaviors focused on spending time together and maintaining connections. "Messing around" centers on the vast amount of information and activity available to teens through the Internet, encompassing trial-and-error investigations, general information seeking, and resource gathering. "Geeking out" encompasses interest-driven behaviors in which youth enthusiastically seek out specific communities of practice and information about narrowly defined topics.

It's not difficult to imagine iCue or something like it opening itself up for such behaviors—allowing for geeking out around stories from the civil rights era or remixing Nixon's farewell with better social-networking support or messing around by supporting creative media commentary on those same events. Moreover, with collaboration and mentorship from site producers and adult members of the community, an environment in which young people follow their own interests in the past through discussion and the production of media could have been glorious. To be sure, there are questions of how to fund such innovations, but the recent disruptions in practices previously believed to be unchangeable, such as the AP History exam and curriculum, may be enough to open opportunities for creative entrepreneurs.

For Every Solution, There Is a Problem

The changes in standards and assessment are both responses and comple-
ments to the research of Ito, Jenkins, and their colleagues, who have found
compelling acts of creation and enthusiasm—acts of learning—in their
work with young people. But there is far from universal agreement that
these changes represent progress. There has been significant backlash
against the notion that the Web enables good learning, and it is important
to take those claims seriously. Emory University English Professor Mark
Bauerlein has advanced the notion that this generation of young people
is *The Dumbest Generation* (Bauerlein 2009):

The technology that was supposed to make young adults more astute, diversify their
tastes, and improve their minds had the opposite effect.

  According to recent reports from government agencies, foundations, survey firms,
and scholarly institutions, most young people in the United States neither read
literature (or fully know how), work reliably (just ask employers), visit cultural
institutions (of any sort), nor vote (most can't even understand a simple ballot).
They cannot explain basic scientific methods, recount foundations of American
history, or name any of their local political representatives. What do they happen
to excel at is—each other. They spend unbelievable amounts of time electronically
passing stories, pictures, tunes, and texts back and forth, savoring the thrill of
peer attention and dwelling in a world of puerile banter and coarse images. (http://
www.dumbestgeneration.com)

These claims are somewhat vague, and it could clearly be argued that these
same limitations of the "current" generation could be (and have been)
leveled at each successive generation by the previous one. Somewhat more
seriously, Duke University researchers Jacob L. Vigdor and Helen F. Ladd
(2010) report that digital technology reinforces the Digital Divide. They
introduced computers into the homes of North Carolina schoolchildren
and observed that those children spent less time on homework and more
time on recreational computer activities such as gaming. As a result, these
students incurred some losses in their reading and math skills. Vigdor and
Ladd acknowledge that there are socioeconomic benefits to learning computer skills, but it seems they chose not to measure those benefits. Further,
David Theo Goldberg (2010), writing on the digital literacy blog DML
Central, highlights an important passage from their study: "One interpretation of these findings is that home computer technology is put to more
productive use in households with more effective parental monitoring, or

in households where parents can serve as more effective instructors in the productive use of online resources. We find evidence consistent with this interpretation." In other words, the same mentoring called for by Ito and her colleagues could have made a difference for Vigdor and Ladd's study subjects. Numerous studies have also debunked that the notion that contemporary students are "digital natives," inherently fluent in any technology but in fact unable to search effectively for information, or create artifacts, thus making another strong case for mentoring (see Ito et al. 2009; Buckingham 2007).

A Casual Model for Success

Although you may need to look closely to see the changing landscape in education, it isn't hard to miss the rapidly changing landscape of online participation and the innovations that have led to that change. In the same time that iCue went from idea to experiment to defunct website, Facebook went from a relatively small niche website for Ivy League grads to the most popular destination on the Internet, valued at $50 billion. Recent Pew numbers (Taylor and Wang 2010) show that 73 percent of online teens are now using social networking, as are 72 percent of eighteen- to twenty-nine-year-olds, up from 55 percent and 50 percent, respectively, in 2006. An even bigger jump is seen in the thirty- to forty-nine-year-olds, who have jumped from 15 percent in 2006 to 39 percent today, representing a potentially friendly teacher audience. Facebook has supplanted MySpace (which announced massive layoffs in 2010).

Facebook has expanded its mission well beyond its initial scope of exchanging pictures and status updates to include hosting applications, aggregating email, and playing games. Meanwhile, Twitter and other social media have been harnessed by young people around the world to facilitate revolutions. On some parts of the Internet, there is an opportunity and an appetite for revolution.

We can gain important insights into the future opportunities for attracting an audience and structuring activities within this space by examining some components of this success. One of the standout successes of Facebook in 2010 was the rapid expansion of social gaming, which brought online games to mass audiences outside the stereotypical adolescent male audience. In 2010, many people declared games such as Farmville and

Sorority Life to be a substantial part of the future of gaming because these models had proved to be such great moneymakers for their respective creators, Zynga and Playdom. Zynga was valued at $5 billion in August 2010 (including a $100 million investment by Google), and Disney bought Playdom for $563.2 million, with a potential $200 million earn-out (Siegler 2010). That same month, Playdom CEO John Pleasants claimed that half of all users of Facebook play social games and that 40 percent of all time on Facebook is spent playing social games. Combine this with a coincident Nielsen Wire report (2010) that claims that 22.7 percent of Americans' time online is spent in social networks (and 85 percent of that time on Facebook in particular) and the picture becomes clear—between 5 and 10 percent of America's online time is spent playing Facebook games. That amounts to almost half of the time that Americans spend playing games online at all, according to that same Nielsen report.

Social gaming seems to appeal greatly to people of all ages. Some "hardcore" gamers may dismiss this market as ineffectual, arguing that these applications are not even games. Games researcher and designer Ian Bogost (2010) was moved enough by this debate to create a game called Cow Clicker, which enables users to log in every four hours or so in order to click on a cow. Unexpectedly, Cow Clicker caught on with several thousand users because the experience is actually kind of fun. In the discussions about these games, perhaps Bogost's colleague Amy Bruckman has the right idea:

Farmville isn't actually a computer *game*—it's a computer *hobby*. In his book *Hobbies*, Steven Gelber [1999] points out that "hobbies developed as a category of socially valued leisure activity in the nineteenth century because they bridged the worlds of work and home" (p. 2). He continues, "before about 1880 a hobby was a dangerous obsession. After that date it became a productive use of free time" (p. 3). Gelber writes:

"As leisure, hobbies provided a respite from the normal demands of work, but as a particular form of *productive* leisure they expressed the deeper meaning of the work ethic and the free market. Hobbies gained wide acceptance because they could condemn depersonalized factory and office work by compensating for its deficits while simultaneously replicating both the skills and values of the workplace, a process I refer to as 'disguised affirmation.'

"Disguised affirmation allows participants to think about an activity as leisure-time recreation while it functions as a form of ideological re-creation. The capacity of hobbies to act simultaneously as resistance and accommodation serves to remind us that we have to examine *all* the meanings of leisure to understand any of them" (pp. 2–3).

I believe we can understand more about why people play games like Farmville by looking hard at stamp collections, sewing circles, and model railroads than by looking at the history of computer "games." Computer "hobby" is a better mental model. (Bruckman 2010)

Bruckman brings us to an interesting point, one that speaks directly to Jenkins's notions of what participatory culture could be, as well as to Gee's notions of affinity spaces. Jenkins reflects on the important history of participatory culture:

My grandmother . . . made quilts, growing up in rural Georgia. We might think of quilting as a kind of remix practice. She took bits of cloth left over from other sewing projects, sometimes drawing on the shared reservoirs of the female community, to create new works. In doing so, she was also building on a shared tradition with its own patterns and formulas. And she was producing an artifact which was designed for sharing—often the quilts were made as gifts to mark social occasions of significance in the life of the community. My grandmother would have known how to engage with a participatory culture.

We can imagine moving from stitching together and remixing textiles to stitching together and remixing media content. . . . In the United States, these folk traditions were radically disrupted by the rise of mass production and mass media. Today, quilt making is a specialized skill, more often trained in art schools than passed along from one generation to the next. And the logic of folk production has become disassociated from our understanding of the media. (Jenkins 2010)

iCue games, as they were originally conceived, shared much of this design philosophy. Although Concentration would be hard to classify as more than a casual game, Connections (also known as Dominoes) could definitely be seen more as a hobby than as a game. Players constructed novel artifacts out of existing resources; each problem didn't necessarily have a right or wrong answer. The players could advance in level of sophistication and explore aspects that were of personal interest. And, like a hobby, the experience extended beyond the playing of the game to discussion with peers about the activity and our shared past. It may be that the era of mass-media disruption has been co-opted (in the case of iCue, by the mass media themselves), opening up opportunities to revisit these ideas. It may also be that our understanding of this kind of game design has advanced enough to make these challenges more manageable and tractable.

Real Value and Real Opportunities

Let us return to the four forms of participatory culture defined by Jenkins and his colleagues that we highlighted in the first chapter: *Affiliations, Expressions, Collaborative Problem-Solving, and Circulations* (Jenkins et al. 2006). All of these activities, devalued by some, still represent the real contemporary practices in fields as diverse as media production and big scientific research (National Research Council 2011). The failure of iCue suggests that education is not quite ready to evolve to accommodate these practices, but we believe it is clear that our society should commit to helping our young people across all walks of life become literate in these practices. Mass media's days are numbered, and mass media are coming to value the coproduction of media with their audiences, and we must continue to encourage them. The big idea for news broadcasters such as NBC News remains that games, media, and online communities could come together to promote engagement with news and civic life. After all, Jones believes that NBC will sustain its news gathering by working in education. Its archives contain droves of valuable material that could be shared for both altruistic and selfish reasons. It could still reach the young audience it craves by realizing that the news is not and never was something that you read in isolation, affecting you alone. Rather it is something that you participate in with a community. In many ways, this could echo the cross-generational "learning centers" described by Collins and Halverson (2009), in which lifelong learners of all ages collaborate and promote each other's self-directed learning.

So will iCue's spirit of connection and its dedication to reshaping how NBC News's audience members think about the stories they see every day, and their education, live on? Will NBC News invest in participatory, distributed education again? Time will tell. For now, it will serve up its archives as a top-down resource (although one still more flexible than a TV channel) and perhaps lie in wait for the next opportunity to innovate, while the field attempts to push that innovation in at the margins and look for the next opportunity to collaborate.

iCue's success is in the eye of the beholder. It failed to reach its intended audience. It never garnered the outside support that it needed to survive and thrive. Many of the initially innovative elements such as games and social networking were not fully realized. It never generated any significant revenue. And before it closed, it never led to an "education revolution." So as a product, it seems as if iCue was a massive failure.

But as we've said, iCue gets to qualify that statement. It changed the organization of NBC News, positioning a major media player in the education market in what was clearly a "disruptive" way. Though the obituary for iCue has been published, it spawned NBC Learn. The product that has emerged from this division is clearly more limited than iCue, yet it has managed to survive and even thrive within a shrinking media industry. A streamlined entity, focusing on access to the archives and the unique personalization that comes with the flippable media player, continues to expand. A recently revamped site has reintroduced some of the participatory elements—but this time among teachers within a community for educators.

Evolution and Revolution

A flippable media player will not revolutionize education. But a media powerhouse, with creativity and without the baggage of a legacy education organization, might help spark that revolution. It can try out new business models that the traditional education companies (textbooks) fear to explore. It can create partnerships with diverse organizations that each bring something to the table, without the need for any single organization to have all of the expertise (and have it already). And they can experiment and innovate, because they don't have any tried-and-true models to which they must stick.

Further, the flippable media player is a significant departure from a traditional text. It is not a predigested presentation of the "facts of history" but rather a presentation of "history's first draft." It is the raw material that students can work with to create their own understanding. And they can flip it over and make it their own. That is a significant departure from the way education is usually practiced (unless things have changed and you're now allowed to write all over your textbooks). Or at least it could be a significant departure if more teachers saw the opportunity to move from a teacher-delivery model to one that incorporates more student-centered activity, and if those students were truly receptive to such a model of participation.

So as a change agent, it seems as if iCue had some success.

We'd like to make the case that this success is purely the result of good, powerful, innovative ideas—that these ideas are the sole operative agent of this story. But they're not. If good ideas in education were all that was needed for an education revolution, academics might have staged a successful revolution years ago. There are a lot of really great ideas that have come from schools of education around the world, and these ideas continue to come. They come in the form of new technologies, new domain-specific pedagogies, models for schools, and methods for student interaction. By and large, these innovations have failed to change education practice significantly. Occasionally, there are shifts in the way people teach particular domains—elementary mathematics, early language acquisition, and so forth. Occasionally, these shifts are even driven by technology, as is the case with calculators, which have changed the way math is taught across grades and topics. In most cases, though, the teacher is still the expert, the blackboard (or smartboard used as a blackboard plus PowerPoint) is still the primary communication medium, and the textbook is the gospel that dictates the curriculum. So why haven't these great ideas revolutionized education practice?

Personalities and partnerships are just as important as ideas.

Personalities

As one of the early iCue players put it, "We exist because of Adam Jones. He was the chief financial officer at the time and those of us who are senior management— we've occasionally wondered about this. I have no idea how Adam got the money together to do this, because he was hiring people and we were starting this project when every other part of the news division was losing people." That is purely a matter of personality. The same goes for the personality of Chisholm. Without his perseverance, resilience, and ability to think across many domains—from the initial educational ideas to revenue and funding models—there would have been no change. When you add in the committed personalities of the believers attracted to the project, both at NBC and at MIT, and Jenkins's dogged work to make ideas popular as a public intellectual, it becomes clear that innovation requires vision and commitment that must be driven by the leadership of some compelling individuals.

Partnerships

Both Chisholm and Jones excel at creating partnerships. Revolution will not come solely from the university. Nor will it come solely from a media conglomerate, or an online university, or a foundation, or a publisher. But together, they can sow the seeds of a revolution—if they are open to change and risk. Effective partnerships spread risk, recruit more resources, bring in diverse expertise, increase reach (and provide a place to point your finger if the project fails!).

Although it can be said that iCue would not have had its impact as a change agent without Chisholm or Jones, it is equally true that it would have floundered without partnerships (some of which nearly brought it down early in its life). The partnership with MIT provided an instant research basis for the project, as well as credibility in the games and social media spaces. Partnerships with distribution agents such as Blackboard and the University of Phoenix ultimately provided the distribution network for NBC Learn that iCue was never able to establish through textbook companies and the College Board. Partnerships with national and private foundations have brought new resources and opportunities to the venture. Even the failed partnership with HotChalk provided some useful insights about how the project might change to serve different markets over time.

With the launch of Education Nation, NBC News is taking its partnerships even further. Collaborations with foundations and corporations have resulted in a significant event, which we are assured will occur annually. This strategy may be viewed as fighting a battle on two fronts. Through

NBC Learn and the Archives on Demand, NBC News has created a product that fits the current marketplace and provides some room for the steady evolution of practices—at least providing teachers with authentic materials to show to students and potentially putting more primary materials directly in the hands of students. At the same time, it is taking the revolution to the streets through Education Nation. Shining a national spotlight on education issues with the help of powerful voices can put pressure on individual organizations and the institution as a whole to change. This combination of approaches may ultimately be the key to success, one that is hard to imagine coming from any other kind of organization.

Change Starts at Home

Back at MIT, we also considered an array of "what if" questions and possibilities. What if we had stayed in our role as game designers and not shifted to research? What if we could have followed through on the participatory media components? What if we had known then what we know now about social gaming? Again, we can't know the answers to these questions, but we have learned from this experiment and have changed our own practices accordingly. Though this project has not dampened our enthusiasm for new media literacies, twenty-first-century skills, and playful, self-directed learning, it also did not have the substantial organizational impact at MIT we might have wished for. For all of the project's advantages, we haven't been able to reduce some of the red tape that makes incubation and innovation difficult. One step at a time.

We have learned the lesson of partnerships. It is *all* about partnerships. We saw what good partnerships provided, what a lack of partnerships drove iCue to at times, and what the consequences of poor partnerships were. Although a good portion of our work still has its foundation in federal funding, we look for partnerships with media production partners, distribution partners, and implementation partners who can do things on a larger scale. We try to partner with for-profits that think about revenue models for sustainability, and whose expertise lends itself to that thinking.

We also saw what sustainability requires. Even though what was sustained in the end was a small fraction of what was originally envisioned, it took an army to do it. We now think about sustainability plans from the onset of projects, even in cases where the money does come in a large chunk from the federal government.

Based on these lessons, we saw the need for an organization outside the university to help us think about sustainability and partnerships. Particularly in the areas of educational games and social media, there are lots of organizations interested in the field, but most of them are ill equipped or unwilling to handle the challenges alone. This situation led to the formation of the nonprofit Learning Games Network (Chisholm and Klopfer are two of the founding members), which helps foster new ideas in the learning games space through partnership building, idea incubation, outreach to students and practitioners, and the development of sustainability models.

The emphasis of the Learning Games Network (LGN) is in fact on the network. This project led Chisholm and Klopfer to two great realizations. The first realization was that *there are a lot of companies, individuals, and nonprofits looking to get into the education game* (and educational games!). The perception of large-scale problems in education, combined with an equally strong perception that there are many opportunities in this arena, has raised substantial interest. Although NBC News's venture alone is evidence of this trend, more evidence arrives every day, such as the previously mentioned purchase of Wireless Generation, a supplier of administrative and curricular computing solutions, by Rupert Murdoch's News Corp. Murdoch, known for having a penchant for pushing technology in traditional industries, clearly believed that there is a lot of money (and changes) yet to be made in education. In Murdoch's case, that meant putting $360 million behind the venture, though if truth be told, he put more than that into the now languishing MySpace (Santos 2010; News Corporation 2010).

The second realization from this experience was that *most of these companies, individuals, and nonprofits know little about schools, teachers, students, or the market forces operating on each of them*. At best, they know only one piece of this puzzle. It is hard to know more than that. But given the volume of interest and the growing expertise in educational media production, particularly in games, more efforts can succeed if the right partners come together. LGN tries to make those partnerships happen through a combination of matchmaking and applying its own experience, management skills, and creativity. Though LGN hasn't taken on any NBC-sized partners yet, it has worked with media producers, smaller broadcasters, foundations, states, and corporations, often at the same time.

As academics, we have had the luxury to think not only of the bottom line; still, we may be starting to see a convergence of cultures from the worlds of academia and corporate media. We see inspiring examples of the ability of corporate media to innovate and take risks. At the same time, academics are increasingly being asked to enlarge the scale of their work and devise sustainability plans to extend the life of their projects beyond the grant-infused capital. This convergence, though fraught with some problems, may actually be beneficial to both sides, and most importantly may provide needed pressure to work together. Slowly but surely, we can work together to help with the evolution of the learning culture, in schools and out, that it seems we all believe our young people need and deserve.

The Takeaway

The biggest and most generalizable takeaway at which we have arrived is that *education is resistant to change from outside—even when that change reflects current real-world trends and is wielded by big companies.* iCue's failure as a product has multiple origins. It never figured out to whom it was marketing itself. It tried to move too quickly to becoming a profitable product. It strayed too far outside the core expertise of the organization. The usage patterns and audience of iCue, combined with the success and observed use of the Archives on Demand, clearly show that teacher-delivered materials are still the norm. Although some teachers venture outside this model, they are the minority, as documented by Groff and Mouza (2008) and Buckingham (2007), among others. Despite the technologically enabled participatory culture of the twenty-first century in which many, if not most, youth engage, this model has not yet penetrated classroom culture on any larger scale. There are many forces pushing against such change, and NBC News struggled against them.

Collins and Halverson argue that in many ways, technologies that are applied in schools are almost always doomed to failure due to the forces at work within the system:

Technologies that require a basic configuration of instructional practice, such as radio or television, are marginalized to preserve school organizations based on text-based media. David Cohen argues that to the degree technology is flexible, it will be adapted to fit that system; to the degree that it is not flexible, it will be ignored or relegated to the periphery. Here, the plasticity of information technologies works against their power to change embedded institutional practices. (2009, 34)

NBC News thought it had cracked this with the introduction of social networks, games, and media to a generation that craved these materials. But alas, in many ways, Collins and Halverson (citing Cohen) were right. The flexible technology (Archives on Demand) is being successfully adapted to the system of schools, and the more prescriptive (in terms of practice) iCue is now ultimately ignored.

So, if NBC News struggles to pull off such change, should we all just throw our hands up in the air and accept the educational status quo? Of course not. Whether through slow *evolution* or more rapid *revolution*, there are ways to innovate in education. And the signs of change in standards and assessment with respect to twenty-first-century skills show promise for creating a more student-centered learning culture. But that change will not come without keeping these ideas in mind:

1. Education is a deceptively complex space and an even more complex marketplace; in order to innovate, you must know who your users are, what you want to do for them, and what they want from you.

There are many players trying to get into the education space, both to make a difference and to make a profit. But education is not a single space. A product designed for student use at home is fundamentally different from a product designed to be used by teachers in schools. Students engage in substantially different kinds of activities in school and out of school, so just knowing what "kids today" are doing is insufficient. Teachers may be interested in many kinds of materials and technologies, but the current system of accountability values a particular set of practices and outcomes that is extremely resistant to change. Not knowing this landscape is what led, at least in part, to the struggles that iCue faced. Figuring out this landscape, and understanding what teachers actually wanted, are also what led to the traction that the NBC Learn Archives on Demand are now getting. These serve the market in a well-defined way that teachers understand, and fit into the current system and practices.

2. Incubation is important. Educational innovation and products require commitment, quality, and lots of recalibration, so a quick turnaround time is a dangerous constraint.

The initial timeline that iCue was operating under was extremely ambitious. The hope was to turn around the site from concept to live rollout in a matter of months. The hope was to make this a "person-hours" problem. With more than sixty producers working full tilt in Studio 3B, they could output thirty person-years of work in just six months. But the problem is that it isn't just a person-hours problem. Getting it right requires not only market research, but actual field testing, feedback, technical infrastructure, marketing, and education. And some of that just takes time. Years later, battle-tested products are starting to emerge from NBC Learn that reflect the lessons of the passage of time. Patience, long-term vision, and some malleability (making allowances for iteration) are important in getting an education product to market.

3. Education is not opposed to new models of participation and interaction, but there are many forces at play (e.g., current standards, accountability) that make such changes difficult. Change can come only when the system is redesigned to accommodate these models.

Teacher-centered delivery via the blackboard at the front of the room, mixed with responses from individual students and occasional small-group work, is the primary mode of operation in most schools and classrooms. Technology is still relegated to one computer at the front of the room (often used to deliver PowerPoint presentations or videos) and isolated computer labs. We know that even today, the activities that students are undertaking when they do get their hands on those computers are largely mundane (Gray, Thomas, and Lewis 2010). There are a lot of kids writing papers on computers but not a lot of them engaging in participatory culture within school. Domain-specific technologies have almost entirely failed to affect classroom practices—possibly only calculators in math, word processors in the humanities, and probeware (digital measuring devices providing real-time data) in the sciences. The world has substantially changed, and the demands on those who graduate from high school and enter the workforce have clearly changed. So too have the practices of students outside school. Many (or perhaps most) teachers would tell you that they'd welcome such opportunities for change in their classrooms, but they can't justify them in the face of the standards and accountability practices that now exist, which don't value innovation. The schools value sure-fire results that bring the known outcomes for which they are accountable. Test-prep software does well in schools these days, as it directly prepares students for the tests that determine student, school, and sometimes teacher outcomes. Those tests value simple, measurable skills. Currently, success involves working within existing constraints while perhaps simultaneously providing external pressure for change. Education Nation may have been just a media event, and it alone clearly is just a drop in the bucket. But as the drops in that bucket accumulate, they apply pressure to change the values in education and adjust the standards and tests to reflect more accurately the demands of the twenty-first century.

4. Private industry, and media companies in particular, have a lot that they can contribute to the educational enterprise (everything from archives to expertise), including an unmatched potential to increase the scale of innovations. But such contributions require collaboration and expertise from other parts of the industry, academia, and the educational enterprise.

NBC News brought a lot to the table as it started on this venture, including not only a vast media archive, but also experience in marketing, a brand name (one that at least parents and teachers recognized), and tremendous resources. Academia values innovation, and many academics have created technologies, products, and approaches that "work" for schools, teachers, and students. They work for the small samples, which may be dozens, hundreds, or—in rare cases—thousands of students. When the funding runs out, we try our best to support the products that we create through additional grants—or simply best efforts. NBC News came with the resources to create and the models to sustain its product. But sustaining meant revenue streams, and public education has an uneasy relationship with paid products beyond textbooks. Textbooks, in turn, have an uneasy relationship with anything digital. Ultimately, what have allowed NBC to sustain its education initiative are the many partnerships it has established. Foundations support new initiatives and provide them free to the public. For-profit educational organizations have valued the materials and brand of NBC News enough to pay for it. And our research program has both contributed to and gained from collaboration. All of these partners are what make this work.

5. There are nonlinearities involved in bringing educational products to a larger scale. Increasing an audience a hundredfold may take a thousand times the work.

It is easy to point to small-scale successful innovations. There are count-less journals on the bookshelf relating their tales. Even those studies that make it to the "large" scale (randomized controlled studies) are small in scale relative to the marketplace. And even those studies entail handpick-ing and negotiating with schools and teachers to make them work. The demands of the educational marketplace, at home and at school, neces-sitate vast resources. Even when a small base of teachers, through the Digital Design Squads and initial launch, were excited, they represented those early adopters. That top few percent is easy to find and attract—it is the next wave of adopters that requires vastly more effort. It is not true that "if you build it, they will come." Sure, there are some cases in which just putting stuff out there on the Web will generate a significant user base. Our colleague Mitch Resnick's project Scratch has managed to do this. (Some good, creative marketing in the MIT Media Lab helped make this possible.) But for every Scratch there are a hundred, or a thousand, or maybe ten thousand projects that fail ever to develop that user base. It takes marketing and distribution channels, outreach, and a lot of effort to make it happen. NBC News put resources into making iCue, but it needed to put in a lot of work, resources, and compromise to attract a significant audience for it.

The Future

Perhaps the most important lesson here is that creating a multimedia website is quite difficult, even if there are media experts from an accom-plished media studies program and a broadcast network with copious content involved. iCue is proof that form and content—even if you believe them to be of the highest caliber—may miss the mark upon a project's debut. Fortunately, the future of NBC Learn more generally seems quite a bit brighter. As Jones described it, as he was departing: "[NBC News] is great for NBC Learn, because the $100 million plus they spend on news gather-ing a year, I get to use for free. It costs me nothing to update, which is why it's an advantage that cannot be competitively met. There's no one that can put 'day of' event video in the classroom like we can. So that's a huge advantage." And it seems as though education, through media pro-duction and media attention, will remain a part of the organization:

I think education has become an important part of what we're doing. So crucially important for NBC News. It has visibility at all levels of the organization now. And I think it's a good thing. *We have a valuable role to play in helping fix the education problem in this country.* It's good business to be in—an area which is so badly needed—and it's "feel good." And everybody here—they're all parents and they get the issues. And it's important to put NBC News as a relevant brand in front of a young audience; it's hard to do anywhere else. It's become an important part of the organization.

While NBC News continues to march on in the direction of educational media sans Jones, we find ourselves back in familiar territory, realizing that perhaps the educational innovation landscape *has* changed in the last five years. We recently had another meeting with representatives from a textbook publisher who wanted to talk with us about partnerships using new media in education. We were fully prepared for the drill once again, for conversations about products that needed to fit state standards and drive textbook sales. But instead, these representatives (with backgrounds in technology, gaming, and media outside the textbook industry) talked about user-generated content, consumer markets, evolution/revolution in schools, and management structures for incubating new ventures within old media organizations. It was as if they'd lived through the lessons of iCue themselves. Whether other textbook companies and education players learn those lessons from this story or others, changes such as that bode well for the future of education and learning.

References

Abram, C. 2006, September 26. Welcome to Facebook, Everyone. http://blog.facebook.com/blog.php?post=2210227130.

Adamic, L., and B. Huberman. 2002. Zipf's Law and the Internet. *Glottometrics* 3:143–150.

APCentral. n.d. AP U.S. History: The DBQ. http://apcentral.collegeboard.com/apc/members/courses/teachers_corner/3497.html.

Barnett, M., K. Squire, T. Higginbotham, and J. Grant. 2004. Electromagnetism Supercharged! In *Proceedings from the 2004 International Conference of the Learning Sciences,* ed. Y. Kafai, W. Sandover, N. Enyedy, A. Dixon, and F. Herrera, 513–520. Mahwah, NJ: Lawrence Erlbaum.

Bauerlein, M. 2009. *The Dumbest Generation.* New York: Penguin Group.

Benevenuto, F., T. Rodrigues, C. Meeyoung, and V. Almeida. 2009. Characterizing User Behavior in Online Social Networks. Paper presented at the Internet Measurement Conference, Chicago.

Bogost, I. 2010. Cow Clicker (computer game). Atlanta, GA.

boyd, d. 2007. Viewing American Class Divisions through Facebook and MySpace. Apophenia blog essay. http://www.danah.org/papers/essays/ClassDivisions.html.

Bruckman, A. 2010, July 26. Farmville as Hobby. Web log comment. http://www.shirky.com/writings/powerlaw_weblog.html.

Buckingham, D. 2007. *Beyond Technology: Children's Learning in the Age of Digital Culture.* Malden, MA: Polity.

Cave, A. 2000. Mattel Sale Ends $3.6bn Fiasco. *The Telegraph.* http://www.telegraph.co.uk/finance/4467013/Mattel-sale-ends-3.6bn-fiasco.html.

Cohen, D. K., and D. L. Ball. 1999. Instruction, Capacity, and Improvement. CPRE Research Report No. RR-043. Philadelphia: University of Pennsylvania, Consortium for Policy Research in Education.

Collins, A., and R. Halverson. 2009. *Re-thinking Education in the Age of Technology: The Digital Revolution and Schooling in America*. New York: Teachers College Press.

Drew, C. 2011, January 7. Thinking Advanced Placement. *New York Times*. http://www.nytimes.com/2011/01/09/education/edlife/09ap-t.html?_r=1&pagewanted=all.

Gee, J. P. 2003. *What Video Games Have to Teach Us about Learning and Literacy*. New York: Palgrave Macmillan.

Gelber, S. 1999. *Hobbies: Leisure and the Culture of Work in America*. New York: Columbia University Press.

Goldberg, D. 2010, August 16. If Technology Is Making Us Stupid, It's Not Technology's Fault. Web log post. http://dmlcentral.net/blog/david-theo-goldberg/if-technology-making-us-stupid-its-not-technology's-fault.

Gray, L., N. Thomas, and L. Lewis. 2010. *Educational Technology in U.S. Public Schools: Fall 2008*. Washington, DC: National Center for Education Statistics.

Greppi, M. 2008, May. NBC News Launches iCue for Students. TV Week. Web blog. http://www.tvweek.com/news/2008/05/nbc_news_launches_icue_for_stu.php.

Groff, J., and J. Haas. 2008. Web 2.0: Today's Technology, Tomorrow's Learning. *Learning and Leading with Technology* 36 (1): 12–15.

Groff, J., and C. Mouza. 2008. A Framework for Addressing Challenges to Classroom Technology Use. *Association for the Advancement of Computing in Education*. 16 (1): 21–46.

Gyarmati, L., and T. A. Trinh. 2010. Measuring User Behavior in Online Social Networks. *The Institute of Electrical and Electronics Engineers Network* (September/October): 26–31.

Hoadley, C. P. 2002. Creating Context: Design-Based Research in Creating and Understanding CSCL. In *Computer Support for Collaborative Learning 2002 Conference*, ed. G. Stahl, 453–462. Boulder, CO: Lawrence Erlbaum Associates.

Horrigan, J. 2006, March 22. For Many Home Broadband Users, the Internet Is a Primary News Source. *Pew Internet & American Life Project*. Washington, DC. http://pewinternet.org/~/media//Files/Reports/2006/PIP_News.and.Broadband.pdf.pdf.

HotChalk. 2010. http://www.hotchalk.com.

Ito, M. 2008. Education vs. Entertainment: A Cultural History of Children's Software. In *Ecology of Games*, ed. K. Salen, 89–116. Cambridge, MA: MIT Press.

Ito, M., S. Baumer, M. Bittanti, D. Boyd, R. Cody, B. Herr, H. Horst, et al. 2009. *Hanging Out, Messing Around, and Geeking Out: Kids Living and Learning with New Media*. Cambridge, MA: MIT Press.

Jenkins, H. 2006. *Convergence Culture: Where Old and New Media Collide.* New York: New York University Press.

Jenkins, H. 2010, June 9. Down Argentina Way. . . . Web log comment. http://henryjenkins.org/2010/06/down_argentina_way.html.

Jenkins, H., P. Ravi, K. Clinton, M. Weigel, and A. Robinson. 2006. Confronting the Challenges of Participatory Culture: Media Education for the 21st Century. http://newmedialiteracies.org/files/working/NMLWhitePaper.pdf.

Jones, S., and S. Fox. 2009, January 28. Generations Online in 2009. Pew Internet & American Life Project. Washington, DC. http://www.pewinternet.org/~/media//Files/Reports/2009/PIP_Generations_2009.pdf.

Joplin, L. 1981. On Defining Experiential Education. *Journal of Experiential Education* 4 (1): 17–20.

K.C.P. Technologies. 2009. Geometer's Sketchpad (software). Emeryville, CA.

Klopfer, E., S. Osterweil, J. Groff, and J. Haas. 2009. Using the Technology of Today in the Classroom Today. *The Education Arcade.* February 2009. http://www.educationarcade.org/node/370.

Klopfer, E., and S. Osterweil. Forthcoming. The Boom and Bust and Boom of Educational Games. *Transactions in Edutainment.*

Laurel, B. 2001. *Utopian Entrepreneur.* Cambridge, MA: MIT Press.

Lageese, D. 2008, May 2. NBC's iCue Brings TV News to a New Generation. *US News and World Report.* Web log. http://money.usnews.com/money/blogs/daves-download/2008/05/02/nbcs-icue-brings-tv-news-to-a-new-generation.

Lenhart, A., S. Jones, and A. Macgill. 2008, December 7. Adults and Video Games. Pew Internet Project Data Memo. Pew Internet & American Life Project. Washington, DC. http://www.pewinternet.org/~/media//Files/Reports/2008/PIP_Adult_gaming_memo.pdf.pdf.

Lenhart, A., and M. Madden. 2005, November 2. Teen Content Creators and Consumers: More Than Half of Online Teens Have Created Content for the Internet; and Most Teen Downloaders Think That Getting Free Music Files Is Easy To Do. Pew Internet & American Life Project. Washington, DC. http://www.pewinternet.org/~/media//Files/Reports/2005/PIP_Teens_Content_Creation.pdf.pdf.

Lenhart, A., M. Madden, A. Macgrill, and A. Smith. 2007, December 19. Teens and Social Media: The Use of Social Media Gains a Greater Foothold in Teen Life as They Embrace the Conversational Nature of Interactive Online Media. Pew Internet & American Life Project. Washington, DC. http://www.pewinternet.org/~/media/Files/Reports/2007/PIP_Teens_Social_Media_Final.pdf.pdf.

Lieberman, D., P. Johnson, and G. Levin. 2006, October 20. NBC Universal Plans Cost Cuts, Layoffs. *USA Today*. http://www.usatoday.com/money/media/2006-10 -19-nbc_x.htm.

Mace, S., and J. Markoff. 1982, September 8. Children Play Games to Learn Basic Skills at TLC. *InfoWorld*: 18–19.

Masie, E. 2008, April 7. Learning TRENDS Podcast: NBC News iCue. Tech-Synergy. Podcast. http://media.masie.com/content/masie/pdf/nbc-podcast_4-7-08.pdf.

Moore, R. J. 2010, January 26. New Data on Twitter's Users and Engagement. Web log. http://info.rjmetrics.com/2010/01/26/new-data-on-twitters-users-and-engagement.

Nagel, D. 2008, May 9. iCue Combines Gaming, Multimedia, Collaboration for Education. *The Journal*. Web log. http://thejournal.com/articles/2008/05/09/icue -combines-gaming-multimedia-collaboration-for-education.aspx.

National Research Council. 2011. *Learning Science through Computer Games and Simulations: Committee on Science Learning: Computer Games, Simulations, and Educations*, ed. M. Honey and M. Hilton. Washington, DC: National Academies Press.

NBC News Billed the Event as Follows. 2010, September 27. Educationnation.com. http://www.educationnation.com.

New London Group. 1996. A Pedagogy of Multiliteracies: Designing Social Futures. *Harvard Educational Review* 66 (1). http://wwwstatic.kern.org/filer/blogWrite44Manila Website/paul/articles/A_Pedagogy_of_Multiliteracies_Designing_Social_Futures .htm.

News Corporation. 2010. News Corporation to Acquire Education Technology Company Wireless Generation. http://www.newscorp.com/news/news_464.html.

Nielsen Wire. 2010, August 2. What Americans Do Online: Social Media and Games Dominate Activity. http://blog.nielsen.com/nielsenwire/online_mobile/what -americans-do-online-social-media-and-games-dominate-activity.

Numedon, Inc. 2011. Whyville Demographics. http://b.whyville.net/top/pdf/ whyville_demographics.pdf.

Papert, S. 1980. *Mindstorms*. New York: Basic Books.

Pew Research Center for the People and the Press. 2004, January 11. Cable and Internet Loom Large in Fragmented Political News Universe. Washington, DC. http://www.people-press.org/2004/01/11/cable-and-internet-loom-large-in -fragmented-political-news-universe/1.

Pew Research Center for the People and the Press. 2011, January 4. More Young People Cite Internet than TV: Internet Gains on Television as Public's Main News Source. Washington, DC. http://people-press.org/files/legacy-pdf/689.pdf.

Power Law. 2012, January 22. Wikipedia. http://en.wikipedia.org/w/index.php?title =Power_law&oldid=472560264.

Rogers, E. 2003. *Diffusion of Innovations*. 5th ed. New York: Free Press.

Roschelle, J., D. Tatar, and J. Kaput. 2008. Getting to Scale with Innovations that Deeply Restructure How Students Come to Know Mathematics and Science. In *Handbook of Design Research in Mathematics, Science, and Technology Education*, ed. A. E. Kelly, R. A. Lesh, and J. Baek. Mahwah, NJ: Lawrence Erlbaum.

Santos, F. 2010, November 23. News Corp., after Hiring Klein, Buys Technology Partner in a City Schools Project. *New York Times*. http://www.nytimes.com/2010/11/24/nyregion/24newscorp.html.

Seiter, E. 2007. *Internet Playground: Children's Access, Entertainment, and Mis-Education*. New York: Peter Lang.

Shirky, C. 2003. Power Laws, Weblogs, and Inequality. http://www.shirky.com/writings/powerlaw_weblog.html.

Sicklos, R. 2005, July 18. News Corp Acquires MySpace.com. http://www.nytimes.com/2005/07/18/business/18cnd-newscorp.html.

Siegler, M. G. 2010, July 30. Half of All Facebook Users Play Social Games—It's 40% of Total Usage Time. http://techcrunch.com/2010/07/30/half-of-all-facebook-users-play-social-games-its-40-of-total-usage-time.

Tancer, B. 2006, July 11. MySpace Moves into #1 Position for All Internet Sites. Hitwise. Web log. http://weblogs.hitwise.com/billtancer/2006/07/myspace_moves_into_1_position.html.

Taylor, P., and W. Wang. 2010, August 19. The Fading Glory of the Television and Telephone. Web log post. Washington, DC: Pew Research Center. http://www.pewsocialtrends.org/2010/08/19/the-fading-glory-of-the-television-and-telephone.

Thomas, D., and J. Brown. 2011. *A New Culture of Learning: Cultivating the Imagination for a World of Constant Change*. Charleston, SC: CreateSpace.

Torres, R. 2010, February 11. 70% of Trial Players Quit WoW before Level 10. http://www.wow.com/2010/02/11/70-of-trial-players-quit-wow-before-level-10.

Tyack, D., and L. Cuban. 1995. *Tinkering toward Utopia: A Century of Public School Reform*. Cambridge, MA: Harvard University Press.

US Department of Education, Office of Educational Technology. 2010. *Transforming American Education: Learning Powered by Technology*. Washington, DC. http://www.ed.gov/sites/default/files/netp2010.pdf.

Vigdor, J., and H. Ladd. 2010. Scaling the Digital Divide: Home Computer Technology and Student Achievement. Cambridge, MA: National Bureau of Economic Research. http://www.nber.org/papers/w16078.pdf?new_window=1.

Vygotsky, L. S. 1978. *Mind in Society*. Cambridge, MA: Harvard University Press.